T0289690

HBR Guide to
Making Every
Meeting Matter

Harvard Business Review Guides

Arm yourself with the advice you need to succeed on the job, from the most trusted brand in business. Packed with how-to essentials from leading experts, the HBR Guides provide smart answers to your most pressing work challenges.

The titles include:

HBR Guide to Better Business Writing

HBR Guide to Building Your Business Case

HBR Guide to Buying a Small Business

HBR Guide to Coaching Employees

HBR Guide to Dealing with Conflict

HBR Guide to Delivering Effective Feedback

HBR Guide to Finance Basics for Managers

HBR Guide to Getting the Mentoring You Need

HBR Guide to Getting the Right Job

HBR Guide to Getting the Right Work Done

HBR Guide to Leading Teams

HBR Guide to Making Every Meeting Matter

HBR Guide to Managing Stress at Work

HBR Guide to Managing Up and Across

HBR Guide to Negotiating

HBR Guide to Networking

HBR Guide to Office Politics

HBR Guide to Persuasive Presentations

HBR Guide to Project Management

HBR Guide to
Making Every Meeting Matter

HARVARD BUSINESS REVIEW PRESS

Boston, Massachusetts

HBR Press Quantity Sales Discounts

Harvard Business Review Press titles are available at significant quantity discounts when purchased in bulk for client gifts, sales promotions, and premiums. Special editions, including books with corporate logos, customized covers, and letters from the company or CEO printed in the front matter, as well as excerpts of existing books, can also be created in large quantities for special needs.

For details and discount information for both print and ebook formats, contact booksales@harvardbusiness.org, tel. 800–988-0886, or www.hbr.org/bulksales.

Copyright 2016 Harvard Business School Publishing Corporation

All rights reserved

Printed in the United States of America

8 2023

No part of this publication may be reproduced, stored in or introduced into a retrieval system, or transmitted, in any form, or by any means (electronic, mechanical, photocopying, recording, or otherwise), without the prior permission of the publisher. Requests for permission should be directed to permissions@hbsp.harvard.edu, or mailed to Permissions, Harvard Business School Publishing, 60 Harvard Way, Boston, Massachusetts 02163.

The web addresses referenced in this book were live and correct at the time of the book's publication but may be subject to change.

Library of Congress Cataloging-in-Publication Data

Title: HBR guide to making every meeting matter.
Other titles: Harvard business review guides.
Description: Boston, Massachusetts : Harvard Business Review Press, [2016] |
Series: Harvard Business Review guides
Identifiers: LCCN 2016025614 | ISBN 9781633692176 (pbk.)
Subjects: LCSH: Business meetings—Handbooks, manuals, etc. | Business meetings—Planning—Handbooks, manuals, etc.
Classification: LCC HF5734.5 .H397 2016 | DDC 658.4/56—dc23
LC record available at https://lccn.loc.gov/2016025614

ISBN: 9781633692176
eISBN: 9781633692183

The paper used in this publication meets the requirements of the American National Standard for Permanence of Paper for Publications and Documents in Libraries and Archives Z39.48–1992.

What You'll Learn

We all know what we're supposed to do to run meetings effectively, but we seldom do them well. Why? Perhaps we think it's just not worth the time to clarify what we hope to accomplish, craft an agenda, handpick participants, issue prework, and send out follow-up notes that detail key decisions and next steps. So we run meetings off the cuff or saddle participants with an overly ambitious agenda we have no hope of working through. Other meeting problems feel beyond our control. People nod their heads in our decision-making meeting but then show their true feelings with their lack of follow-through. Derailers. Latecomers. Blowhards. Nonparticipants. People who bring *their* agenda to *your* meeting.

The best way to prevent or overcome any of these obstacles is thoughtful and thorough preparation. This guide offers tips and scripts for curbing inappropriate behavior and making your meetings easier to prepare for, more efficient to conduct—and more productive.

You'll learn how to:

- Determine whether you even need to meet
- Prepare a realistic agenda

- Identify why you're meeting—and articulate your purpose to attendees

- Orchestrate group decision making

- Prevent implementation roadblocks by giving participants equal airtime

- Cope with chronic latecomers, windbags, and other people problems

- Turn around a bad meeting

- Run any type of meeting—from a status stand-up to a one-on-one walking check-in to a strategy off-site

- Get the most out of digital meeting tools

- Hold people accountable without hounding or micromanaging

- Keep the momentum going with prompt meeting follow-up

Contents

Contents

SECTION TWO

Conduct

SECTION THREE

Participate

Contents

SECTION FOUR

Close and Follow Up

SECTION FIVE

Specific Types of Meetings

The Condensed Guide to Running Meetings

by Amy Gallo

Editor's note: Here's where to start if you need to organize a meeting soon—and you don't have a ton of time to prepare, but you want to do it right. When you're not so pressed for time, take a look at the rest of the book, which expands on themes raised here.

We love to hate meetings. And with good reason—they clog up our days, making it hard to get work done in the gaps, and so many feel like a waste of time.

Adapted from content posted on hbr.org on July 6, 2015.

Paul Axtell, author of *Meetings Matter: 8 Powerful Strategies for Remarkable Conversations,* says that this is a major pain point for nearly every manager he works with. "People are absolutely resigned," he says. "They have given up on the hope that it could be different." Axtell and Francesca Gino, author of *Sidetracked: Why Our Decisions Get Derailed, and How We Can Stick to the Plan* and a professor at Harvard Business School, weigh in here on whether much of the conventional wisdom on meetings holds true.

"Keep the meeting as small as possible. No more than seven people."

Though research does not point to a precise number that's ideal, "there is evidence to suggest that keeping the meeting small is beneficial," says Gino. For one thing, you're better able to notice body language when there are fewer people. "In a group of 20 or more, you can't keep track of the subtle cues you need to pick up," says Axtell. And if you want people to have the opportunity to contribute, limit attendance. In Axtell's experience, limiting it to four or five people is the only way to make sure everyone has the chance to talk in a 60-minute meeting.

The challenge with large meetings isn't just that everyone won't have a chance to talk but that many of them won't feel the need to. "When many hands are available, people work less hard than they ought to," explains Gino. "Social psychology research has shown that when people perform group tasks (such as brainstorming or discussing information in a meeting), they show a sizable decrease in individual effort from when they perform alone." This is known as "social loafing" and tends to get worse as the size of the group increases.

That's not to say that your 20-person meeting is doomed for failure. You just need to plan more carefully. "The degree of facilitation has to go up," says Axtell. You have to be more thoughtful about getting input from the group and reading people in the room. "You need someone who is masterful at managing the conversation."

"Ban devices."

Both experts agree this is a good idea, for two reasons. First, we know devices distract us. Gino points out that many people think they can multitask—finish an e-mail or read through their Twitter feed while listening to someone in a meeting. But research shows they really can't. "Recent neuroscience research makes the point quite clear on this issue. Multitasking is simply a mythical activity. We can do simple tasks like walking and talking at the same time, but the brain can't handle multitasking," says Gino. "In fact, studies show that a person who is attempting to multitask takes 50% longer to accomplish a task and makes up to 50% more mistakes."

And those who pick up their devices during meetings may well be the worst multitaskers. "The research finds that the more time people spend using multiple forms of media simultaneously, the less likely they are to perform well on a standardized test of multitasking abilities," explains Gino.

The second reason to ban devices is that they distract others. Gino recently conducted a simple survey that assessed whether people thought reaching for a phone, posting a status on Facebook, or writing a tweet during a meeting was distracting or socially inappropriate. The subjects "found the same action to be much more problematic if their friend or colleague engaged in it but did not find it to be very problematic when they were the ones who were (arguably) being rude," she says. These results suggest that we feel annoyed when others are on their devices during a meeting. "Yet we fail to realize that our actions will have the same effect on others when we are the ones engaging in them," she says. This is what Axtell sees in practice: People feel insulted when someone reaches for their phone, especially if that person is a senior leader. "If you're presenting or talking about an idea, and you see a senior manager on their phone, it hurts," he says.

Still there are some good reasons to use technology in a meeting, says Axtell. You may want to take notes or retrieve reference material. "Perhaps they need to be available because something important is going on in their lives," he says. But if these circumstances don't apply to your participants, have everyone turn their devices off and pay attention.

"Keep it as short as possible— no longer than an hour."

Research shows that there are advantages to keeping meetings short. One reason is that people stay more focused during shorter time spans. "Classic studies have found that groups adjust both their rate of work and their style of interaction in response to deadlines and time constraints," says Gino. For example, one study showed that "groups solving problems communicated at a faster rate and used more autocratic decision-making processes under high time pressure than they did when time pressure was low."

"Once people realize you're tight on time, they stop asking questions or talking and focus on getting the work done," says Axtell.

This doesn't mean you should try to cram every meeting into a 30-minute slot. Axtell warns that there are conversations that necessitate more time, and you shouldn't rush over certain topics. "If the purpose of your meeting is to talk through something, you need to give people enough time to voice their opinions, build on one another's ideas, and reach a conclusion," he says. Time pressure will make this more efficient, but you don't want to make the time so short that you truncate important conversations (chapters 6 and 7 offer suggestions for ideal meeting length).

"Stand-up meetings are more productive."

While some might feel that stand-up meetings are a gimmick, Gino points out that there is empirical data that proves they work. In one study (done in 1999 before stand-up meetings were a staple in most offices), Allen Bluedorn from the University of Missouri and his colleagues concluded that stand-up meetings were about 34% shorter than sit-down meetings, yet they produced the same solutions. (For a different take on stand-up meetings, see chapter 29.)

Axtell finds these types of solutions encouraging. "I like that people are trying to do something bold to change up meetings—going for a walk, standing up," he says. But, he warns, don't let the format distract you from doing what really matters: running an effective meeting. "I'd prefer people have the guts to say 'I'm going to run this meeting well.'"

"Make sure everyone participates, and call on those who don't."

Some people may want to speak up in your meeting but feel like they can't unless they're asked, says Axtell. This may be due to "cultural reasons, or language barriers, or general disposition." Axtell believes that people who hold back often have the best perspective on the conversation, and you need to draw them out.

Having everyone contribute isn't just good for the end result of your meeting, it's good for the participants as well. People like to know that their opinions are being heard and considered, says Gino. And "just by asking people in the meeting for their opinion, you're going to raise their commitment to the issues being discussed."

For people you know may feel too put on the spot, talk to them ahead of time and tell them that you're hoping they'll contribute. That way they'll have time to plan what they'll say. Then in the meeting, you may still need to prompt them by asking for their perspective, but they'll be primed to do so.

"Never hold a meeting just to update people."

"If you're already meeting for worthwhile topics, it's okay to give a quick update," says Axtell. You might ask at the end if there's anything the group needs to be aware of or if there's something going on in the department that others need to know about. "But if you're only meeting to transfer information, rethink your approach," Axtell urges. "Why take up valuable time saying something you could just send in an email?"

Wasting time isn't the only problem with update meetings. Gino explains that research by Roy Baumeister, Kathleen Vohs, and their colleagues suggests that we have a limited amount of what they call "executive resources." "Once they get depleted, we make bad decisions or choices," says Gino. "Business meetings often require people to commit, focus, and make decisions with little or no attention paid to the depletion of the finite cognitive resources of the participants—particularly when the meetings are long or too frequent." She finds that in her own research, "depletion of our executive resources can even lead to poor judgment and unethical behavior." So if you can avoid scheduling yet another meeting, you should.

"Always set an agenda ahead of time, and be clear about the purpose of the meeting."

It's hard to imagine more sound advice about meetings. Axtell and Gino agree that designing the meeting and setting an agenda ahead of time is critical. "You should explain what's going to happen so participants come knowing what they're going to do," says Axtell. In her book, *Sidetracked,* Gino talks about how lacking a clear plan of action is often why groups get derailed in decision making. "Having a plan gives us the opportunity to clarify our intentions and think through the forces that could make it difficult for us to accomplish our goals," she says.

Following the advice given here will ensure that the next time you need to bring a group together, you'll make it a good use of everyone's time—including your own.

———————

Amy Gallo is a contributing editor at *Harvard Business Review* and the author of the *HBR Guide to Dealing with Conflict*. She writes and speaks about workplace dynamics. Follow her on Twitter @amyegallo.

SECTION ONE

Prepare

CHAPTER 1

Do You Really Need to Hold That Meeting?

by Elizabeth Grace Saunders

"Let's schedule a meeting" has become the universal default response to most business issues. Not sure what to do on a project? Let's schedule a meeting. Have a few ideas to share? Let's schedule a meeting. Struggling to take action? Let's schedule a meeting.

Although scheduling a meeting can be the right solution in many instances, it's not always the best answer. Here's a decision tree to help you quickly determine if holding a meeting makes the most sense (see figure 1-1).

Adapted from content posted on hbr.org on March 20, 2015.

FIGURE 1-1

Should I hold a meeting?

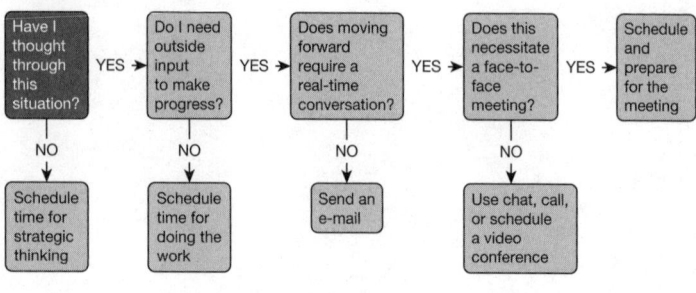

Copy this decision tree, and keep it handy. It makes it quick and easy to decide whether or not to hold a meeting. Here's what you should consider at each step.

Have I thought through this situation?

When you don't have clarity about what you're doing on a project, it's tempting to schedule a meeting to give you the feeling that you're making progress. But unless the meeting's intent is to structure the project, scheduling a meeting is probably an inefficient use of your time—and your colleagues'. Instead, do some strategic thinking. Evaluate the scope of the project, its current status, and the potential milestones, and lay out a plan of action for making meaningful progress. Once you've completed your own strategic thinking prep work you can consider if it makes sense to hold a meeting.

Do I need outside input to make progress?

You may be in a situation where you know what needs to be done, and you simply need to do the work. If so, don't schedule a meeting; update your to-do list, and take action instead. However, if after clarifying what needs to be done you require outside input to answer questions or give feedback before you feel comfortable jumping into action, continue on.

Does moving forward require a real-time conversation?

If you have questions that need to be answered but don't require a two-way conversation, e-mail can be an excellent alternative to a meeting. This is particularly true when you're looking for feedback on your written plans or documents. It's much more efficient for everyone involved if you send over items that they can look at on their own (while you're not awkwardly watching them read during an in-person meeting) and then shoot you back feedback. If you feel your situation does require a real-time conversation, examine different communication channels.

Does this necessitate a face-to-face meeting?

When you need two-way communication but don't necessarily need to see the person, you have a variety of options. An online chat can help you answer questions quickly, or for more in-depth conversations, scheduling a phone call or video conference can work well. This not only saves you the transition time of going to and from a meeting place, it also allows you to continue working if someone is late, rather than having to sit somewhere and wait for them to show up.

If in the end you decide that you need face-to-face, in-person communication, then schedule a meeting, and think through in advance how you can make it as efficient and effective as possible. That means considering your intent for the meeting, establishing your desired outcomes, and preparing any materials that should be sent out or reviewed in advance.

This decision-making process can help you radically reduce the number of meetings you attend and increase the amount of work that gets done.

Elizabeth Grace Saunders is the author of *How to Invest Your Time Like Money* (Harvard Business Review Press, 2015), a time coach, and the founder of Real Life E Time Coaching and Training. Find out more at the website www.RealLifeE.com.

CHAPTER 2

Stop Calling Every Conversation a "Meeting"

by Al Pittampalli

When both a 500-attendee event and a two-person discussion are referred to as "meetings," it's difficult to suss out a gathering's true purpose and to know how to prepare to make it successful. In order to have fewer, more purposeful meetings, we need a more robust vocabulary to describe them. So let's do some renaming, starting with three common "meetings" that you'll soon realize aren't really meetings at all.

Meetings with just two people are actually **conversations**. Whereas meetings with ample attendee lists

---

Adapted from content posted on hbr.org on November 3, 2015.

require an agenda, plenty of preparation, and an artic-
ulable purpose, one-on-one discussions need not be as
rigorous. They aren't weapons of mass interruption, and
humans are naturally good at them. So keep conversations casual, and hold them as often as you'd like.

Another kind of meeting that needs to be renamed
is one in which work actually gets done. Management
expert Peter Drucker famously noted that a "working meeting" was impossible: "One either meets or one
works. One cannot do both at the same time." And, for
the most part, he's right. Most meetings involve planning
and coordinating the work, not executing it. But sometimes people—writers, programmers, mathematicians—
do huddle around a laptop or whiteboard to do real work
together. Let's call these **group work sessions** and make
sure to disinvite the bureaucrats.

Then there are meetings where the primary goal is to
generate ideas. If you want people to be truly imagina-
tive and express themselves, don't dare call it a brainstorming meeting. Just call it a **brainstorm**. Since these
sessions are designed to maximize creativity, it's a good
idea to play a warm-up game, get people standing and
active, and give people permission to have fun—free
of judgment and criticism. If someone walks past the
conference room and thinks you're having a "meeting,"
you're probably not doing it right.

Now let's consider a few types of meetings that are
difficult to justify if you name them correctly. Take, for
example, meetings that are called primarily because
managers have information to disseminate. Rather than
distributing a memo or having several one-on-one con-

versations, these bosses decide to save time by wasting the time of their colleagues, disrupting work, and corralling the team into a room together. These are **convenience meetings** and almost always a bad idea. They're typically convenient for the individual and inconvenient for everyone else.

Meetings called as a matter of tradition or habit—**formality meetings**—should also be banned. These gatherings may have served a purpose at one time but do so no longer. Rather than considering an issue and asking "Is a meeting the best way to address it?" we treat the event as a given and ask "What issues do we need to address at this meeting?" This ensures we always find things to discuss, no matter how trivial they are.

Some meetings are called under the guise of collaboration or alignment when it's really connection we're after. These are **social meetings**. Connection is a laudable goal, but meetings are a pretty lousy way to foster it. Instead, invite people to a team-building activity, a retreat, or a party. But make it optional. While the extroverts on the team might love the chance to socialize, the introverts may want to stay back and get some work done.

Finally, we come to the **decision-making meeting**, a total misnomer as it implies that the meeting itself is making the decision. But meetings don't make decisions; leaders do. Group discussions can help support that process, of course, so let's rename these types of gatherings **decision-supporting meetings** to remind the leader that it's her job, and hers alone, to make sure action follows. It's also helpful to distinguish between high-stakes, low-stakes, and no-stakes decision-supporting meetings.

In a high-stakes meeting, you want to facilitate a real honest debate. Research shows that moderate task conflict leads to more accurate decisions, so demand candor from attendees, and encourage them to disagree. Identifying these meetings as high-stakes will remind you to let the best decision prevail, even if it's not yours.

When the decisions to be made are less consequential, the goal isn't to slow down, it's to speed up. Propose a plan for moving forward, and focus on generating buy-in. Of course you should allow for disagreement and be prepared to revise your plan if participants offer good reasons. But aim for quick resolution so you can spend most of the time coordinating implementation. As for meetings called to support inconsequential, no-stakes decisions? They should obviously never see the light of day.

Imagine a culture where people regularly talk about meetings using this kind of precise language. Picture someone pushing back on a meeting invitation by calling it a formality meeting. Envision the leader of a decision-supporting meeting asking whether her gathering qualifies as high stakes or low stakes. Think about someone canceling an upcoming staff meeting and requesting a few conversations instead. Better language isn't the only step you must take to transform your meeting culture, but it's a powerful start.

Al Pittampalli is the author of *Persuadable: How Great Leaders Change Their Minds to Change the World* (HarperBusiness, 2016).

CHAPTER 3

If You Can't Say What Your Meeting Will Accomplish, You Shouldn't Have It

by Bob Frisch and Cary Greene

How many times have you walked out of a theoretically important meeting—a leadership off-site, a C-suite pow-wow, a sit-down with the board—thinking, "That was a great discussion, but I'm not sure we really accomplished anything?" More often than not, the problem lies not in

Adapted from content posted on hbr.org on April 18, 2016.

what did or didn't happen at the meeting itself but in the fact that you didn't get anything done because the goals for the meeting were never firmly established in the first place.

We see this happen all the time when clients hire us to help manage off-sites. Often, they start by handing us a pretty well-developed (and usually packed) agenda full of already-booked speakers and a finalized list of confirmed attendees. Beyond logistics, the actual substance of the off-site is nearly set. But then we always ask the meeting owner—the most senior executive hosting it—the same two questions:

- What do you want to have debated, decided, or discovered at the end of this session that you and the team haven't already debated, decided, or discovered?

- What do you want attendees to say when their team members ask, "What happened at the big meeting?"

In almost every case, the response is the same: "That's a good question—I hadn't actually thought about those things."

It doesn't matter if it's an 8-person board meeting, a 15-person executive team meeting, a 150-person leadership conference, or a regularly recurring status meeting: Your first step when planning an important meeting should be to draft an initial set of goals based on the answers to the two questions above. In the words of Stephen Covey, "Begin with the end in mind." These objectives are not the activities you will be engaged in or the time slots on the agenda. They are more high level: your desired outcomes for the meeting.

The list needn't be very long or complicated. As a starting point, three to five short bullet points or sentences that articulate what you want to accomplish is more than enough.

But this process may take some time. You could go through two to three iterations before you have a straw-model set of objectives that are ready to be tested with other key meeting stakeholders, who should then be asked to review the list and identify any missing or unnecessary goals. Once everyone is aligned, agree and communicate to all other attendees that these objectives are locked in. This will help keep the agenda focused and give you cover if someone asks to add an unrelated presentation or discussion at the last minute.

Here are some sample objectives from different types of meetings we've facilitated recently.

Regularly recurring weekly meeting

- Share updates and review progress-to-date, including major milestones or upcoming activities (ask and answer "What did I do? What will I do?").

- Identify questions and concerns related to progress (ask and answer "What are the potential roadblocks?").

- Prioritize and resolve issues and address additional questions.

- Agree on next steps (for example, escalation of issues, clear accountabilities, etc.).

Board meeting

- Provide board input as management formulates the new five-year strategy.

  - Agree on how much runway remains on the current core strategy.

  - Identify new strategies to potentially pursue.

- Finalize the operating model for strategic governance.

  - Launch annual strategic planning process.

  - Put in place long-term (five-plus-year) strategic oversight.

- Agree on the topics and timing for additional board input into the current planning cycle.

Executive team meeting

- Develop a list of growth opportunities for the team to assess further.

- Begin to define select growth opportunities, including the future-state description for each and potential measures of success.

- Confirm the accountable executive and team leader for each opportunity.

- Understand the time line and activities over the next three months.

Leadership conference

- Establish the purpose and positioning of the extended leadership team.

- Impart a meaningful understanding of the company's vision, mission, and strategy, including top priorities for the next three years.

- Understand priority issues raised by attendees, and develop potential solutions.

- Align around next steps.

Your list of objectives must also drive important decisions about aspects of the meeting.

Agenda. Draft an agenda, and map each activity to your stated goals. Do all of them help you achieve one or more of your objectives? Are there any objectives that can't be achieved through what you have planned?

Attendees. The number and identity of attendees should be based on the scope and objectives of the meeting. For example, if you need to make decisions, we recommend a smaller group. If your aim is to generate ideas or achieve broad organizational buy-in for an initiative, you should invite a larger group.

Pre-reads. Don't overload people with voluminous meeting pre-reads full of assorted plans, reports, and studies that aren't directly related to your objectives. Instead, use your list to organize, filter, and focus the content you send in advance.

Location. The location of your meeting should reflect its objectives, too. For example, if your goals focus on a specific region, go there. If an explicit objective is for participants to get to know each other better, pick a venue designed for socializing.

When you set out and share your objectives in this way, it ensures that everyone is "coming to the same meeting." Attendees will be energized and ready to accomplish those goals.

Bob Frisch is the managing partner of the Strategic Offsites Group, a Boston-based consultancy, and is the author of *Who's In The Room? How Great Leaders Structure and Manage the Teams Around Them* (Jossey-Bass, 2012). He is the author of four *Harvard Business Review* articles, including "Off-Sites That Work" (June 2006). **Cary Greene** is a partner of the Strategic Offsites Group. They are coauthors of *Simple Sabotage: A Modern Field Manual for Detecting & Rooting Out Everyday Behaviors That Undermine Your Workplace* (HarperOne, 2015) and are frequent contributors to hbr.org.

CHAPTER 4

How to Design an Agenda for an Effective Meeting

by Roger Schwarz

An effective agenda sets clear expectations for what needs to occur before and during a meeting. It helps team members prepare and allocate time wisely, quickly gets everyone focused on the same topic, and makes it clear when the discussion is complete. If problems occur during the meeting, a well-designed agenda promotes the team's ability to address them right away.

Here are some tips for designing an effective agenda for your next meeting. You'll find sample agendas and

---

Adapted from content posted on hbr.org on March 19, 2015.

a blank template in appendix B. These suggestions will be helpful whether your meeting lasts one hour or three days or whether you're meeting with a group of five people or forty.

Seek input from team members. If you want your team to be engaged in meetings, make sure the agenda includes topics that reflect their needs. Ask team members to suggest agenda items and an explanation of why each area needs to be addressed in a team setting. If you ultimately decide not to include an item, be accountable: Explain your reasoning to the team member who suggested it.

Select topics that are relevant to the entire team. Team meeting time is expensive and difficult to schedule. It should mainly be used to discuss and make decisions on issues that affect the whole team—and that need the whole team to solve them. These are likely to be areas in which individuals must coordinate their actions because their parts of the organization are interdependent. They are also likely to be issues for which people have different information and needs. Examples might include: How do we best allocate shared resources? How do we reduce response time? If the team isn't spending most of the meeting talking about interdependent issues, members will disengage and ultimately not attend.

List agenda topics as questions the team needs to answer. Most agenda items are simply several words strung together to form a phrase, such as: "office space reallocation." This leaves meeting participants wondering, "What about office space reallocation?" When you list a topic as a question (or questions) to be answered, it instead reads like this: "Under what conditions, if any, should we reallocate office space?"

A question enables team members to better prepare for the discussion and to monitor whether their own and others' comments are on track. During the meeting, anyone who thinks a comment is off track can say something like, "I'm not seeing how your comment relates to the question we're trying to answer. Can you help me understand the connection?" The team knows that when the question has been answered, the discussion is complete.

Note whether the purpose of the topic is to share information, seek input for a decision, or make a decision. It's difficult for team members to participate effectively if they don't know whether to simply listen, give their input, or be part of the decision-making process. If people think they are involved in making a decision, but you simply want their input, everyone is likely to feel frustrated by the end of the conversation. Updates are better distributed—and read—prior to the meeting, with a brief part of the meeting allocated to answering participants' questions. If the purpose of the topic is to make a decision, state the decision-making rule. If you're the formal leader, at the beginning of the agenda item you might say, "If possible, I want us to make this decision by consensus. That means that everyone can support and implement the decision given their roles on the team. If we're not able to reach consensus after an hour of discussion, I reserve the right to make the decision based on the conversation we've had. I'll tell you my decision and my reasoning for making it." (For more on group decision making, see chapter 12.)

Estimate a realistic amount of time for each topic. This serves two purposes. First, it requires you to do the math: to calculate how much time the team will need for introducing the topic, answering questions, resolving different points of view, generating potential solutions, and agreeing on the action items that follow from discussion and decisions. Leaders typically underestimate the amount of time needed. If there are 10 people in your meeting and you have allocated 10 minutes to decide under what conditions, if any, you will reallocate office space, you have probably underestimated the time. By doing some simple math, you would realize that the team would have to reach a decision immediately after each of the ten members had spoken for a minute.

Second, the estimated time enables team members to either adapt their comments to fit within the allotted time frame or to suggest that more time may be needed. The purpose of listing the time is not to stop discussion when the time has elapsed; that simply contributes to poor decision making and frustration. The purpose is to get better at allocating enough time for the team to effectively and efficiently answer relevant questions.

Propose a process for addressing each agenda item. A defined process makes it possible to identify the steps the team should take to complete a discussion or make a decision. Agreeing on a process significantly increases meeting effectiveness, yet leaders rarely do it. Unless a team has agreed on a process, members will, in good faith, participate based on their own process. You've probably seen this in action: Some team members are trying to define the problem, while other team members are wondering why the topic is on the agenda, and still other members are already identifying and evaluating solutions.

The process for addressing an item should appear on the written agenda. When you reach that item during the meeting, explain the process and seek agreement. For example: "I suggest we use the following process. First, let's take about 10 minutes to get all the relevant information on the table. Second, let's take 10 minutes to identify and agree on any assumptions we need to make. Third, let's take another 10 minutes to identify and agree on the interests that should be met for any solution. Finally, we'll use about 15 minutes to craft a solution that ideally takes into account all the interests and is consistent with our relevant information and assumptions. Any suggestions for improving this process?"

Specify how members should prepare for the meeting. Distribute the agenda with sufficient time before the meeting so the team can read background materials and prepare their initial thoughts for each agenda item ahead of time.

Identify who is responsible for leading each topic. Someone other than the formal meeting leader can be responsible for leading the discussion of a particular agenda item. This person may provide context for the topic, explain data, or have organizational responsibility for that area. Identifying this person next to the agenda item ensures that anyone who is responsible for leading part of the agenda knows it—and prepares for it—before the meeting.

Make the first topic "review and modify agenda as needed." Even if you and your team jointly developed the agenda before the meeting, take a minute to see if anything needs to be changed due to late-breaking events. I once had a meeting scheduled with a senior leadership team. As we reviewed the agenda, I asked if we needed to modify anything. The CEO stated that he had just told the board of directors that he planned to resign and that we probably needed to significantly change the agenda. Not all agenda modifications are that dramatic, but by checking in at the beginning of the meeting, you increase the chance that the team will use its meeting time most effectively.

End the meeting with a plus delta evaluation. If your team meets regularly, two questions should form a simple continuous improvement process: What did we do well? and What do we want to do differently for the next meeting? Investing 5 or 10 minutes will enable the team to improve performance, working relationships, and team member satisfaction. Here are some questions to consider when identifying what the team has done well and what it wants to do differently.

- Was the agenda distributed in time for everyone to prepare?

- How well did team members prepare for the meeting?

- How well did we estimate the time needed for each agenda item?

- How well did we allocate our time for decision making and discussion?

- How well did everyone stay on topic? Did team members speak up when they thought someone was off topic?

- How effective was the process for each agenda item?

To ensure that your team follows through, review the results of the plus delta evaluation at the beginning of the next meeting.

If you develop agendas using these tips, your team will have an easier time getting—and staying—focused in meetings.

———————

Roger Schwarz is an organizational psychologist, speaker, leadership team consultant, and president and CEO of Roger Schwarz & Associates. He is the author of *Smart Leaders, Smarter Teams: How You and Your Team Get Unstuck to Get Results* (Jossey-Bass, 2013). For more, visit www.schwarzassociates.com or find him on Twitter @LeadSmarter.

CHAPTER 5

The Key to Shorter, Better Meetings

by Anthony Tjan

Your meetings may often cut across multiple objectives, but setting and articulating the purpose of your meeting will help participants prepare and contribute more effectively. Outside general relationship-building, consider that a business meeting has only three functional purposes:

1. To inform and bring people up to speed.

2. To seek input from people.

3. To ask for approval.

Adapted from content posted on hbr.org on June 23, 2009.

Use this as a filter to determine why you're having a meeting, to clarify your agenda viewing items through this lens, and to explain your purpose to your audience.

Consider a meeting that sets its agenda goals along the lines of "I want to bring you up to speed on these two things," or "I need input on this item," or "I would like to get your approval on these outstanding issues." That's it: a simple, three-purpose rule that frames the goals of the meeting from the perspective of each participant.

Anthony Tjan is CEO, managing partner, and founder of the venture capital firm Cue Ball. He is coauthor of *Heart, Smarts, Guts, and Luck: What It Takes to Be an Entrepreneur and Build a Great Business* (Harvard Business Review Press, 2012).

CHAPTER 6

The 50-Minute Meeting

by David Silverman

I have a life-changing proposal for businesspeople everywhere: 50-minute hours. Start a productivity revolution by scheduling business meetings that, by default, run 50 minutes long instead of 60.

How often do you find that by 11 a.m. you're running late, and by 3 p.m. you've either been forced to dump a meeting to reset your day or are 100 e-mails behind because you've gone straight from one appointment to another all day long? Either way, you're leaving someone (or many people) in the lurch. It's a stressful and unsatisfying existence.

Adapted from content posted on hbr.org on August 6, 2009.

There's another group of people who are scheduled in back-to-back sessions all day long, five days a week. I speak, of course, of students. All the way through school we're taught in 50-minute blocks, a schedule that lets us get to our next class on time. The buildings even have bells to remind the person running the meeting—er, class—to end on time.

Why is it, then, that when we graduate, they take away our bells, replace them with an irritating "doink" sound signaling "15 minutes until your next meeting," and assume we can now teleport to the next location? What could cause such madness? In two words: Microsoft Outlook. (Not without blame would also be IBM Notes, Google Calendar, Apple's Calendar, and others.)

By default, Outlook sets up meetings that are 30, 60, 90, or 120 minutes long. There's no room for travel time, to compose yourself, to answer a couple of e-mails, or for a coffee or bathroom break.

Next time you're faced with scheduling a meeting, consider booking a 20-minute or 50-minute session. See what you can accomplish in that time, and if you can still get to your next meeting. You may just start a new trend in your organization.

David Silverman has been an entrepreneur, an executive, and a business-writing teacher. He is the author of *Typo: The Last American Typesetter or How I Made and Lost 4 Million Dollars* (Soft Skull Press, 2009).

CHAPTER 7

The Magic of 30-Minute Meetings

by Peter Bregman

Often we schedule one-hour time slots. Why? How did an hour become our standard time allotment for so many meetings, phone calls, and appointments? Recently I tried a new experiment: I cut the time I allot for many activities in half.

I started with something easy. I used to work out for an hour a day. Now it's down to 30 minutes. My results—weight and conditioning—improved.

Adapted from content posted on hbr.org on February 22, 2016.

Here's why: My intensity is higher (I know I only have 30 minutes), I eat better (I don't rely on my workout to keep slim), I integrate movement more into my day (I don't rely on my workout to take care of all my fitness needs), and I never miss a workout (I can always find 30 minutes).

If you have half the time to accomplish something, you become hyperaware of how you're using that time. And hyperfocused during it. Most of my meetings are now 30 minutes or less. My podcast is 15 to 20 minutes. Even many of my conference calls, with multiple parties, are 30 minutes or less. People on the calls, aware of the time constraint, are more thoughtful about when they speak and more careful not to follow tangents that aren't useful.

People also listen better because when things are moving faster, we tend to be more alert. We know that a single distracted moment will leave us behind. And, since that keeps us more engaged, we end up having more fun in the process.

Nowhere has this impact been more transformational —and more evident—than in the leadership coaching we do at Bregman Partners. For the past several years, all of our coaching is accomplished in 30-minute sessions. The advantages are obvious: Everyone saves time and money. But here's what's less obvious: The coaching isn't simply as powerful as what we could do in a longer session, it's vastly more so. When the coach and the client both know they have only 30 minutes, they move into high gear.

- **People show up.** Just as with my workouts, clients are far less likely to skip a 30-minute session than they are an hour-long one.

- **Everyone is on time.** Every minute counts in a 30-minute conversation, and people know it. The session gets started more quickly, because everyone's aware that the relationship is built on doing good work, not on making small talk.

- **People are much more likely to come prepared.** There's no time wasted on off-topic items and going-nowhere conversations. Clients know what they want to cover and have put some thought into it beforehand.

- **The time pressure enhances focus and attention.** People don't focus on multiple issues; they tackle the single biggest opportunity or most persistent, intractable obstacle. And they move on it.

- **Coaches are more willing to be courageous, and clients are more willing to be prodded.** In a 30-minute session, coaches can't waste time beating around the bush. They get to the point faster and earlier, interrupt more bravely, and ask more provocative questions.

The compressed, focused coaching session hones the skill of getting to the point quickly, focusing on the most essential elements of a situation, and taking action. The downside? I haven't seen one yet. Try it yourself. Transition some of your hour-long meetings to

30 minutes. As you do, consider these three steps as a way to make the 30 minutes most powerful:

1. Read what you need to beforehand, and tell everyone else to do the same. Think about your questions and concerns. Decide what's important to you and what you can let go of. Ask yourself the most important question: What outcome do you want?

2. Decide on the one thing that will make the biggest difference, and spend the 30 minutes on that issue, topic, or opportunity. Get started right on time, no matter who isn't there, and be bold and disciplined at keeping the conversation on track. Let go of anything that is less critical. Make decisions quickly, even if they are imperfect. Getting traction on a single thing is far more useful than touching on many issues without forward momentum on any.

3. Save at least the last five minutes to summarize what you learned, articulate what was valuable, commit to what you're going to do as a result of the meeting, and clarify how you'll assess the success of your next steps. The sign of a great meeting isn't the meeting itself—it's what happens after that meeting.

Like our coaches, you'll need these "get to the most critical point fast" skills—and the courage to use them—if you're going to make the most of your time. You need to be bold and even provocative. You need to be willing to interrupt, thoughtfully and for the greater good of moving ambitiously toward what is most important. You need to let go of things that don't really matter.

And you need to be fully present. No multitasking. No texting under the table. No distractions. Which is also the upside: you get to be fully present in what you are doing.

There is a cost. While it's energizing, it also takes a lot of energy to be so focused, even for a short amount of time. It's a sprinter's tactic.

On the other hand, when you cut your meetings in half, you'll have a lot more time to relax at dinner, write, sleep, and spend unstructured time with people you love.

Peter Bregman is CEO of Bregman Partners, a company that strengthens leadership in people and in organizations through programs (including the Bregman Leadership Intensive), coaching, and by consulting with their CEOs and leadership teams. He is the best-selling author of *18 Minutes* (Business Plus, 2011), and his most recent book is *Four Seconds* (HarperOne, 2015).

CHAPTER 8

Meetings Need a Shot Clock

by Bob Frisch and Cary Greene

We've all been invited to meetings with agendas so long that it's impossible to cover every item. The early speakers run long. The early proposals get debated. But those at the end get short shrift or are tabled until the next gathering, even if they're equally important.

How can you avoid this problem? One option is to limit your ambitions, to be more realistic about what you can get done in the hour or hours you're meeting. Simply resign yourself to covering less. In our view, however, there's a better solution, one that allows you to accomplish more while still ensuring that each person or topic gets adequate time. As crazy as it sounds, the answer is

Adapted from content posted on hbr.org on March 16, 2016.

a shot clock. Yes, an actual shot clock, like the ones they use in high school, college, and professional basketball games. The NBA and the NCAA put the shot clock in place years ago to quicken the pace of play, because some teams (especially when leading near the end) passed the ball endlessly without penalty. Now there's a limit on the time a team has to shoot—24 seconds in the NBA, 30 seconds in the NCAA—and if that time runs out, the ball goes to the opponent.

We've experimented with the same system in business meetings—especially when fair process is important to uphold—and had great success. Although most attendees tend to be a bit skeptical at first, they quickly recognize the purpose and value of the shot clock: It ensures that all agenda items are covered and each is allocated appropriate time.

Here's how it works: Before a meeting begins, explain that you want to devote a certain amount of time to each topic. For example, if you're leading an annual budget review and have 40 investment proposals on the table, you might say, "We're going to spend exactly 10 minutes on each topic. Speakers will have three minutes to present, followed by seven minutes of discussion."

Of course, sometimes different topics require different amounts of discussion time. A relatively straightforward issue might warrant five minutes, while a more contentious one merits 20. If you can identify the more time-consuming items in advance, great. If not, consider using a few minutes at the start of a meeting to determine how much time each agenda item deserves. One organization we worked with listed topics on a wall chart and asked attendees to put a green, yellow, or red dot next to each one to signify whether it deserved 7, 10, or 15 minutes of discussion, respectively. To limit the number of 15-minute conversations, each person only had three red dots to dole out.

Once you've determined appropriate time allocations, set up the shot clock. A smartphone stopwatch works nicely. It should buzz—loudly—when time runs out and keep buzzing until the person stops talking.

When people are introduced to this tool, they usually both love it and hate it. They like the fact that it limits others from commandeering too much time, overanalyzing decisions, and beating dead horses in debates, but they don't enjoy getting cut off themselves. Still, we often find that by the end of that first meeting, everyone has grown more comfortable with it and even fond of it. The shot clock is impersonal—even obnoxious—but that's what makes it effective. It's fair. Everyone is guaranteed to get a turn, and each issue is given the attention it needs. No one gets to "buy" extra floor time because of their status. It grants no wiggle room.

The shot clock also keeps meetings lively, focused, and sharp. And it's a great training tool. At several meetings, we've observed that executives who are tasked with speaking on multiple agenda items progressively get better at managing the clock. The first time they might run a tad over. The second time they come in right at the buzzer. By the third or fourth time, they're expressing themselves much more succinctly and wrapping up well before their minutes run out. They are more careful with their time because—just like the best basketball players—they know it's fixed.

———————

Bob Frisch is the managing partner of the Strategic Off-sites Group, a Boston-based consultancy, and is the author of *Who's In The Room? How Great Leaders Structure and Manage the Teams Around Them* (Jossey-Bass, 2012). He is the author of four *Harvard Business Review* articles, including "Off-Sites That Work" (June 2006). **Cary Greene** is a partner of the Strategic Offsites Group. They are coauthors of *Simple Sabotage: A Modern Field Manual for Detecting & Rooting Out Everyday Behaviors That Undermine Your Workplace* (HarperOne, 2015) and are frequent contributors to hbr.org.

CHAPTER 9

Are There Too Many People in Your Meeting?

When you set up a meeting, the people you invite are just as important as what you need to get done.

It may be easy to default to inviting a crowd of people to a meeting—that way, you don't really have to identify the most critical participants, you can avoid any ruffled feathers, you'll have everyone involved on hand for a decision, and you won't have to repeat your communications separately afterward. Or maybe your tendency is to keep things small, to invite just a handful of people whose opinions you value most.

Adapted from content posted on hbr.org on March 18, 2015 and from *Running Meetings* (20-Minute Manager series; product#17003), Harvard Business Review Press, 2014.

But for a meeting to be most useful, you have to have the right people—and only the right people—in the room. With too many attendees, you might have trouble focusing everyone's time and attention and not accomplish anything; with too few, you might not have the right decision makers or information providers in the room.

As you plan your attendee list, consider who will help you accomplish your meeting's goal and who will be most affected by its outcome. You'll likely want to include a combination of people who will offer a variety of perspectives. Take the time to methodically list each individual and place them into the following categories to make sure you include the right people:

- The key decision makers for the issues involved

- Those with information and knowledge about the topics under discussion

- People who have a commitment to or a stake in the issues

- Those who need to know about the information in order to do their jobs

- Anyone who will be required to implement decisions made

Consult with other stakeholders to make sure you've made the right list. Often another key stakeholder can remind you of a perspective you forgot to bring into the room.

Just because someone's name is on your list, however, doesn't mean they must be at the meeting. How many people should you actually invite? There are no hard-and-fast rules, but in principle, a small meeting is best for deciding or accomplishing something, a medium-sized meeting is ideal for brainstorming, and a large meeting makes the most sense for communicating and rallying. Some people use what's known as the 8–18-1800 rule as a rough guideline:

- If you have to solve a problem or make a decision, invite no more than 8 people. If you have more participants, you may receive so much conflicting input that it's difficult to deal with the problem or make the decision at hand.

- If you want to brainstorm, then you can go as high as 18 people.

- If the purpose of the meeting is to provide updates, invite however many people need to receive the information. However, if everyone attending the meeting will be providing updates, limit the number of participants to no more than 18.

- If the purpose of the meeting is for you to rally the troops, go for 1,800—or more!

If you decide not to invite individuals you listed as likely to be affected by the meeting's outcome, have a plan to communicate the substance of the meeting to them afterward.

Conduct

CHAPTER 10

Before a Meeting, Tell Your Team That Silence Denotes Agreement

by Bob Frisch and Cary Greene

The meeting seemed to go smoothly. Bill, the executive vice president of sales at a global company, had gathered his extended leadership team—a group of more than 20 people—and outlined his latest plan to reconfigure the sales organization. When he asked if anyone had

Adapted from content posted on hbr.org on February 3, 2016.

concerns, there were a few questions, but no one raised any significant obstacles or issues, and some of the more senior team members spoke up in support of the plan. Bill felt that everyone was on board and ready to go.

But later that week, one of the meeting attendees came into Bill's office. "Do you remember when you were talking about reconfiguring the sales organization?" the attendee asked. "I'm not sure we've got Latin America quite right." Similar scenes played out with other direct reports and more-junior employees in the halls and cafeteria over the next few days. People had opinions they hadn't shared at the meeting. The plan, which had seemed unanimously popular, was now unraveling. What happened?

Most bosses assume that when they directly ask for feedback, people will offer their thoughts candidly. It's great when that happens. But it often doesn't, especially in public settings and high-stakes situations. If you get unanimous, but mostly unvoiced, support for a decision that you thought might be contentious, it should be a warning sign.

Why do people hold back from weighing in? In some cases, junior people may hesitate to disagree with bosses or senior colleagues. In others, the most powerful team members may be disinclined, for political or other reasons, to express candid opinions in front of the group because they know they can always get access to decision makers or launch a covert campaign to sway support their way after the fact.

How can you prevent this from happening? Set one key ground rule: Silence denotes agreement.

These three words do a great job of forcing people to open up, no matter how reluctant they may be feeling (or how passive-aggressive they are). Explain to people that if they don't say anything when given a proposal or plan, they're voting "yes" for it. Silence doesn't mean "I'm not voting" or "I reserve the right to weigh in later." It means "I'm completely on board with what's being discussed."

You must then commit to enforcing the rule. If someone—even a powerful team member or friend—comes up to you after a meeting to express reservations about what was said, the response should be "You should have spoken up at the meeting. Now everyone is on board and the ship has sailed. Next time, say something."

Sometimes the establishment and reinforcement of "silence denotes agreement" as a ground rule is enough to get the opinions flowing. But if you sense that some participants are still finding it difficult to express themselves freely, consider the following tactics, which allow perspectives to be aired in a way that focuses on the ideas rather than on the individuals voicing them.

- **Take anonymous polls.** Ask people to write down questions or concerns on index cards, put them into a bowl, and read them aloud without using names. Better yet, use a polling app or device to query meeting participants and see their answers in real time.

- **Heat map the topic.** Put poster-sized charts of the components of an idea or plan on the wall. Ask participants to place yellow dots on the charts where they have a question and red dots where they have a significant concern. Use the dots to guide the conversation.

- **Break up a big group.** People are more likely to participate in small group discussions, so divide people into teams with specific instructions to discuss any challenges to the proposal at hand. Appoint a representative from each group to summarize everyone's thoughts.

- **Ask them to empathize.** People are often more willing to speak on others' behalf than on their own. So when you solicit opinions with a question like "What objections or concerns might your direct reports have?" it can open the floodgates of reaction. That's because it allows those in the room to externalize criticism. It's not what they don't like. It's what they think their *people* won't like.

When you enforce the discipline of "silence denotes agreement" and use the tactics described here, everyone is motivated to say what they really think immediately and discuss it openly, rather than flagging problems after the fact.

Bob Frisch is the managing partner of the Strategic Off-sites Group, a Boston-based consultancy, and is the author of *Who's In The Room? How Great Leaders Structure and Manage the Teams Around Them* (Jossey-Bass, 2012). He is the author of four *Harvard Business Review* articles, including "Off-Sites That Work" (June 2006).

Cary Greene is a partner of the Strategic Offsites Group. They are coauthors of *Simple Sabotage: A Modern Field Manual for Detecting & Rooting Out Everyday Behaviors That Undermine Your Workplace* (HarperOne, 2015) and are frequent contributors to hbr.org.

CHAPTER 11

Establish
Ground Rules

Setting guidelines at the beginning of a meeting encourages everyone's participation and keeps the conversation on track. The guidelines don't have to be rigid or overly formal but should serve as a set of shared expectations for behavior that reflect your time constraints, the size of your group, and your meeting's intentions and goals. For example, your group may decide to let only one person speak at a time, not allow interruptions, set time limits on contributions, table issues that aren't easily resolved, limit conversations that stray from the topic at hand, and make sure that everyone is heard from.

Adapted from *Running Meetings* (20-Minute Manager series; product #17003), Harvard Business Review Press, 2014; and Martha Craumer, "How to Run an Effective Meeting: The Basics."

If you're meeting with the same group of people on a regular basis, the group can develop these guidelines together. Otherwise, suggest some ground rules at the beginning of your meeting, and get buy-in from the attendees.

Specifying ground rules signals to participants that you intend to keep things moving efficiently.

- Reassert that you're committed to beginning and ending on time (and then really do it).

- Ask for everyone's participation and openness to new ideas.

- Agree to listen to each other and limit interruptions—and as the leader, enforce that rule.

- Clarify how decisions will be made. Let the group know right up front if this will be a group-decision meeting, a meeting that calls for participants' input, or a meeting that shares a decision that has already been made.

- Explain your policy on multitasking and device use.

You may also need to establish ground rules for specific agenda items:

- Clarify constraints that exist for any issue that will be under discussion—for example, upper-management decisions or policy or budget restrictions that may limit the group's range of options.

- Identify the final decision maker for each item—
  especially if it's not someone in the meeting (such
  as the CEO or department manager).

Martha Craumer is a senior writer at The Boston Consulting Group.

CHAPTER 12

Reach Group Decisions During Meetings

Facilitating group decisions in meetings is rarely easy. The following suggestions for choosing the right decision-making method will help ensure that everyone leaves your meetings with clear decisions and next steps for implementing those decisions.

You can use three common decision-making methods with groups: group consensus, majority vote, or leader's choice. Each has its own benefits and challenges.

Adapted from *Running Meetings* (20-Minute Manager series; product #17003), Harvard Business Review Press, 2014.

Group Consensus

Group consensus does not mean arguing and lobbying until everyone agrees. It means reaching a decision that everyone understands, supports, and is willing to help implement.

Advantages:

- Allows all meeting participants to share their expertise in order to arrive at the best decision.

- Results in all participants understanding the decision and its implications.

- Greatly enhances the chance for buy-in from all parties.

Disadvantages:

- Participants may not be familiar with this decision-making process: They may think that they all have to agree to and believe in the final outcome, so it may feel like people are spinning their wheels or heading in the wrong direction.

- May take more time than other decision-making approaches.

- May require that you have an alternative decision-making process (for example, leader's choice) in case consensus cannot be reached within given time constraints.

How do you know when you have a genuine consensus? You'll hear comments such as "Option A isn't my first choice, but I believe it incorporates everyone's needs." Or "I don't think Option A satisfies all our criteria, but I'm prepared to implement it as fully as possible."

Majority Vote

The proposal or idea with the most votes wins.

Advantages:

- The group arrives at a decision relatively quickly.

- The group perceives the decision to be fair.

- You hear from everyone, even people who are usually quiet.

Disadvantages:

- Open voting requires taking public stands on issues and can result in perceived winners and losers.

- People may not feel comfortable voting according to their true feelings or voicing reservations they might have about decisions.

- Losers often feel their voices have not been heard.

- Not everyone buys into the decision.

Leader's Choice

In some ways, having the leader decide is similar to a majority rule because the leader needs to hear what the participants think and is most likely to agree with the majority view.

Advantages:

- It's the fastest approach to decision making and may be the best approach when time is short or when there is a crisis.

- If the meeting participants respect the leader and understand why they are making a certain decision, people are somewhat more likely to buy into the decision.

Disadvantages:

- Meeting participants may feel that the leader is ignoring their views, particularly if they haven't been given the chance to state their ideas.

- You may encounter resistance during implementation, as meeting participants may feel less ownership or may not have bought in completely.

CHAPTER 13

The Right Way to Cut People Off in Meetings

by Bob Frisch and Cary Greene

You've spent hours preparing for the meeting. The objectives are clear. The agenda is tight. Relevant material was distributed to attendees in advance. Smartphones are put away, and your team seems focused and ready to work.

The conversation begins, but after 10 minutes of good discussion on the first agenda item, someone goes off on a tangent that, while interesting, is only marginally related to the designated topic. Then another person jumps in to elaborate, and the two start talking in detail

---

Adapted from content posted on hbr.org on April 8, 2016.

about issues relevant only to them. Other attendees begin to tune out. Now 20 minutes have passed—and you haven't made any progress.

We've all seen scenes like this play out, whether in an hour-long meeting or at a multiday off-site. Participants veer off topic or take the conversation into the weeds, and because no one feels comfortable doing anything about it, critical agenda items are left untouched. In fact, research suggests that "getting off the subject" is the number one challenge to meeting productivity. When leaders or peers do try to intervene, it's often after too much time has passed (since they've waited for the perfect opportunity to interrupt), and the typical approach—"This is really interesting, but can I suggest we get back to the topic at hand?"—leaves everyone feeling awkward.

Thankfully, there is a simple solution to this predicament: the word "jellyfish." Jellyfish are, of course, those funny-looking creatures with no brain, no blood, and no heart that have drifted along on ocean currents for millions of years. We use the word to prevent meetings from drifting.

Here's how it works. At the start of your gathering, introduce the jellyfish ground rule: If any attendee feels the conversation is heading off course or delving into an inappropriate level of detail, they can and should employ the word to indicate that opinion. Simply say "jellyfish" or "I think we're having a jellyfish moment" or "Gee, did I just see a jellyfish swim by?" It's a catchall for "Why don't you take this offline—the rest of us would like our meeting back."

Of all things, why is "jellyfish" so effective?

It's safe. The word is both simple and funny, and if set up correctly at the start of a meeting, it carries the same effect as other, more traditional (and less comfortable) ways of interrupting and redirecting the conversation. Of course, you can pick another, similarly silly word, but we've been using this one for years and have found that people—indeed, entire organizations—quickly embrace it.

It's accessible. Anyone can invoke it. The meeting owner or facilitator may be the first to use it, but they don't have to be the only one. Any participant can ask, "This feels like jellyfish. Do you agree?" prompting the person or people on the tangent to ask themselves if they are using the group's time well.

It raises awareness. When meeting participants know that jellyfish will be used, they can't help but become more self-aware about staying on topic. In many cases we've even seen attendees call jellyfish on themselves.

In decades of helping clients conduct better meetings, we've found "jellyfish" to be one of the most effective ways of keeping the discussion on target.

Bob Frisch is the managing partner of the Strategic Offsites Group, a Boston-based consultancy, and is the author of *Who's In The Room? How Great Leaders Structure and Manage the Teams Around Them* (Jossey-Bass,

2012). He is the author of four *Harvard Business Review* articles, including "Off-Sites That Work" (June 2006). **Cary Greene** is a partner of the Strategic Offsites Group. They are coauthors of *Simple Sabotage: A Modern Field Manual for Detecting & Rooting Out Everyday Behaviors That Undermine Your Workplace* (HarperOne, 2015) and are frequent contributors to hbr.org.

CHAPTER 14

Dealing with People Who Derail Meetings

by Roger Schwarz

What does your team do when someone takes a meeting off track? If your team is like most, the leader says something like, "Lee, that's not what we're talking about now" or "Let's get back on track" or the team simply ignores Lee's comment and tries to bring the conversation back to the original topic.

But if your team responds in any of these ways, Lee may continue to press his off-topic point, the meeting may drag on with members getting more frustrated with

---

Adapted from content posted on hbr.org on September 20, 2013.

Lee, and the team may not accomplish its meeting goals. Or Lee may stop participating for the rest of the meeting and the team, without realizing it, will lose Lee's critical input and support for implementing a team decision.

If you assume that Lee or others who derail a meeting are the problem and the solution is to get them back on track or stop them from talking, you may be off track. These team members' behaviors are often a symptom of larger team problems. People often make off-track comments when there isn't clear agreement on the meeting's purpose or process, or when the team doesn't provide time to hear everyone's thoughts on a topic. Sometimes the problem is that you think others are off track when they aren't. So what should you do?

Agree on the track before going down it.

If your team doesn't explicitly agree on the purpose and topic for each part of the meeting, then people will use their own understanding to decide what is appropriate. Because team members will naturally have different interpretations, one person's comments can easily seem off track to others.

Start your meeting by saying something like, "My understanding of the purpose of this meeting is X; does anyone have a different understanding or think we need to add anything?" This ensures that if people think other issues need to be addressed, they can say so and have them considered for the agenda, rather than raising them as off-track items. If it's not your meeting and there is no agenda, simply ask "Can we take a minute to get clear on the purpose and topics for the meeting to make sure we accomplish what you need?"

Check that others are ready to move down the track.

Rather than saying "Okay, let's move on" or simply shifting to a new topic, say something like "I think we're ready to move to topic Y. Anyone have anything else we haven't fully addressed on X?" If some people aren't ready to move on, find out what needs to happen before they can move forward. This reduces the chance that people will raise issues later that you thought had been fully discussed. If your team is staying focused but regularly runs out of time before completing its agenda, then you're underestimating the amount of time necessary to make high-quality decisions that generate commitment. When you and the team agree on the goals and make sure everyone is ready to move on, you're jointly designing next steps, and that builds commitment to decisions.

Test your assumption that the meeting is getting derailed.

If the team has agreed on the topic to discuss and you still think that someone is off track, say something like, "Lee, I'm not seeing how your point about outsourcing is related to the topic of our planning process. Help me understand the connection." When Lee responds, you and other team members might discover a link between the two topics that you hadn't considered. For example, Lee might say that outsourcing will free up internal resources so that the team can complete the planning process in less time. If there is a connection, the team can decide whether it makes more sense to explore Lee's idea now or later. If it turns out that Lee's comment isn't related but is still relevant for the team, you can suggest placing it on a future agenda. One caveat: There are times when it is critical to address team members' issues immediately, even if they're off track. If team members raise highly emotional issues about how the group is working together, it's important to acknowledge the issue's importance and then decide whether it's more essential to address it than the current agenda topic. Sometimes focusing on how the team works together is more critical than sticking with the team's substantive topics.

This is more than a polite way of dealing with people who get off track: It's a way to suspend your assumption that you understand the situation and others don't, to be curious about others' views, and to ask people to be accountable for their own contributions so that the team can make an informed choice about how best to move forward. For this approach to work, you can't just say the words; you have to believe that Lee's topic might be connected and that you don't see it.

By getting explicit agreement about the meeting's purpose and topics and by being genuinely curious when people seem off track, you and your team can move faster and accomplish more in your meetings.

Roger Schwarz is an organizational psychologist, speaker, leadership team consultant, and president and CEO of

Roger Schwarz & Associates. He is the author of *Smart Leaders, Smarter Teams: How You and Your Team Get Unstuck to Get Results* (Jossey-Bass, 2013). For more, visit www.schwarzassociates.com or find him on Twitter @LeadSmarter.

CHAPTER 15

Refocus a Meeting After Someone Interrupts

by Rebecca Knight

You did everything you were supposed to do: invited all the right people, sent out an agenda in advance, and got everyone's agreement on the process. But despite your diligence, your meeting is being hijacked. How should you handle a persistent interrupter? Will it work to just ignore the person? And how can you regain control of the meeting?

Adapted from content posted on hbr.org on April 16, 2015.

What the Experts Say

Whether it's a team member who disagrees with your approach, an employee from another department who brings up irrelevant information, or a colleague who wants to use your meeting as a soapbox for their own personal agenda, dealing with interrupters during a meeting is challenging. "When someone interrupts you, blocks you, or otherwise thwarts your intended action, it's natural to feel upset," says Judith White, visiting associate professor at Dartmouth's Tuck School of Business. "This is a basic instinct, and you will always have a flash of annoyance." The key to successfully dealing with interrupters is to quash your frustration and instead "operate from a mind-set of curiosity," says Roger Schwarz, an organizational psychologist and the author of *Smart Leaders, Smarter Teams.* Here's how to handle disruptors and regain control.

Gather Input Ahead of Time

"A well-designed agenda both provides a structure for the meeting and serves as a point of reference," Schwarz explains. People are less likely to disrupt a meeting if they feel like they had a hand in shaping it. So send out a proposed agenda ahead of time, and ask your team for input. Give them a time frame for making recommendations, and ask that they include a reason why they think an item is worthy of discussion. Everyone should have a say, but "the team leader gets the final decision about what to include." While an agenda does not entirely prevent interruptions, "it becomes the basis of your intervention," says Schwarz. Once you're in the meeting, if someone interrupts with an off-topic remark, Schwarz suggests saying something like, "I don't see how your comment connects to the issue we're talking about now. Help me understand how the two relate." If the speaker can't draw a connection, "then you use the agenda to pick up where you left off," he says.

Stay Calm

When someone interrupts or challenges you in a meeting, manage your response. "Don't get emotional" says White. "If you look threatened or angry, you will lose the trust of everyone in the room." Rather, your goal should be to "react with humor, kindness, inclusion, and assertiveness." Modulate your tone of voice and inflection, too. When you respond to the person who is interrupting, Schwarz says, "Speak in a genuinely curious, not frustrated, way."

Listen, Validate, Redirect

Don't be tempted to ignore the interruption and move on. At the point of interruption, "you need to stop talking and listen to what the person has to say," White explains. Then summarize his points "to let him know he's been heard." Let's say, for instance, you're leading a meeting about new corporate initiatives, and your colleague, Bob, interjects with, "Why are we bothering to discuss this? We don't have money in the budget to execute these ideas." You should then say, "Bob, your point is that we don't have money in the budget for this. And that's a good point." After validating his comments, redirect the discussion. Start by restating the purpose of the meeting. In this instance, White suggests you could say something along the lines of, "We have great minds in this room, and the president of our company asked us to work together to come up with cost-efficient ideas. I am confident we can do it."

Probe Further

Don't always rush to redirect the conversation, however, warns Schwarz. It's not necessarily your goal to move through the meeting agenda as quickly as possible. Rather, he says, your aim is to "address issues efficiently, but also in a way that leads to a sustainable solution. When a colleague interrupts you with a comment you think is off topic, that's not a fact; it's an inference." Ask your colleague to elaborate on his point. if you're still unsure how what he's saying relates to the topic at hand, ask others at the meeting for help. Frame the interruption as "an opportunity for learning a new perspective," he says. "Think: What does he know that I don't know?" It may be that he has a perspective you haven't thought of. Says Schwarz: "Take time to address legitimate issues, because they're not going away."

Be Resolute and Direct

When a colleague persists in interrupting, is off on a tangent, or keeps on making the same point over and over, be direct and firm, says White. She suggests saying something like "Rich, you've brought this issue up before, and we heard you. If you would like to stay after the meeting and talk with me, I'd be happy to discuss the matter further, but now we need to get back on track." Or you could directly address the colleague who keeps on interrupting. Schwarz recommends a script like this: "Bob, I'm seeing a pattern, and I'm trying to figure out what's happening here. Is there something going on that's leading you to bring up these items?" While some might contend that this strategy puts Bob on the spot, Schwarz says "you need to deal with the issue in the place where the data lies—within the team." Handling situations in the open also allows you to model to your team how to have challenging conversations and provides a forum for others to add relevant information.

Use Body Language to Take Back Control

When your meeting is in danger of derailment because of insistent or hostile interrupters, regain control using body language and nonverbal communication. "If you're already standing, take a step or two toward the person who's interrupting you," says White. "Face that person and hold his gaze for five seconds—it will feel like an eternity." Never cross your arms. "You should appear open," she says. Then, walk slowly around the table, "stand directly behind the person who's disrupting the meeting, and address the rest of the room." Proceed accordingly. This, of course, requires confidence and finesse. Even though it's not always easy, "it's a powerful way to exert influence," she says.

Consider Having a One-on-One Conversation

After a meeting filled with tense and numerous interruptions, you might spend a little time alone reflecting on

WHEN A SIT-DOWN IS CALLED FOR

Sometimes nothing you do in a meeting will help break someone of their problematic behavior. If this is the case, sit down with that person and speak directly with them. Here are tips for approaching the encounter.

1. *Ask permission.* "May I talk to you about today's meeting?"

2. *Clarify goals.* Ask the person what they hope to get out of the meeting. Discuss what you see as the meeting's core goals.

3. *Describe the behavior.* "I see you doing *X*." This way, you each have a common reference point.

4. *Describe the consequences.* Explain how the behavior is affecting the group's performance,

whether you're doing anything to contribute to the problem, says Schwarz. It might also be worth approaching the interrupter for a one-on-one conversation. "Don't argue with him after the meeting, and never scold," says White. "He wants to feel heard." Instead, pose questions and listen. Ask: What is your thinking on this issue? What would you like done differently? What's important to you? "It may turn out that you both want the same thing, in which case, propose that you become allies," she says. On the other hand, "you can agree to disagree." (See

and detail the consequences you see it having for the group.

5. *Inquire about the root of the behavior.* Ask, for example, if the person is upset about a particular issue.

6. *Make a specific suggestion or request.* "At the next meeting, please try not to dismiss an idea until others have had a chance to finish their thoughts." Being unambiguous increases the likelihood that they will change their behavior.

7. *Agree on next steps.* Getting the person to commit to changing their behavior will help them actually do so.

Adapted from *Harvard Management Communication Letter* (product #C0504B), Spring 2005.

the sidebar "When a Sit-Down Is Called For" for more ideas on conducting this conversation.)

———————

Rebecca Knight is a freelance journalist based in Boston and a lecturer at Wesleyan University. Her work has been published in the *New York Times, USA Today,* and the *Financial Times.*

Participate

CHAPTER 16

Polite Ways to Decline a Meeting Invitation

by Liane Davey

There it is in your inbox: an invitation to a meeting you really don't want to attend. Maybe because it's shoe-horned into one of the few open spaces in your calendar. Or perhaps it's at a time that's already booked, and now you're left to decide whom to turn down. Sometimes you just need to click "decline."

Your first challenge is deciding which meetings to say no to. Establish a set of criteria for participation, and stick with it. Ask yourself the following questions.

Adapted from content posted on hbr.org on May 17, 2016.

What is the value of the meeting?

Start by assessing whether the meeting is about something important, timely, and worthwhile. Is it set up for success by having a clear purpose and an agenda? Is there background information available to inform participants in advance? Are the appropriate people invited so that meaningful progress can be made? If the value of the meeting isn't clear from the invitation, reply back with a few open-ended questions before making your decision:

- "Could you please provide some additional information on the agenda?"

- "What stage of decision making are we at on this topic?"

- "How should I prepare for the discussion?"

Am I the right person to attend?

If it's clear that the meeting is worthwhile, your next question is whether or not you should be there. Are the issues within the purview of your role? Do you have the expertise to contribute to the conversation? Are you underqualified or overqualified for the level of decision making on the table? If you're questioning why you were invited, reach out to the meeting organizer before responding:

- "What are you looking for me to contribute at this meeting?"

- "Who else will be there from my department?"

- "Who will I be representing?"

Is the meeting a priority for me right now?

If you believe the meeting will be valuable and that you would make a contribution to the discussion, consider how it aligns with your goals and work. How central is the meeting topic to your role? Where does the issue fit relative to your other immediate demands? How unique is your contribution, and could your seat be better filled by someone else?

If you ask yourself these questions and find that your participation isn't essential, then it's appropriate to decline the meeting. Even if you choose not to attend, the following options can help you demonstrate that you're a good team player and a positive contributor, even if you can't be in the room.

Can I stop the meeting altogether?

If the meeting failed your first criteria because you don't believe it's set up for success, talk with the organizer about your concerns. It's possible the person will dismiss your comments, but you could also trigger one of two positive outcomes: Either the meeting gets better positioned for success or gets cancelled. Try one of the following approaches:

- "This is an interesting topic. Based on our current-year priorities, I'm not sure we're ready for a productive conversation yet. Would it be possible to push this meeting back and let the working group make a little more progress before we meet?"

- "I'm looking forward to making some decisions on this issue. From the meeting invite, it doesn't look like Production is involved. I would like to wait until someone from that team is willing to join. Otherwise, we won't be able to make any decisions."

- "Based on the information in the invitation, it looks like this meeting is for informational purposes. Would it be possible to get a summary sent out rather than hold a meeting?"

Can I recommend someone else?

If the meeting is important, but it failed your second criteria because you're not the right person for the job, try nominating someone else. Invest some effort in finding the right person so you don't appear to be shirking the responsibility. Try floating these options:

- "I'm glad that you're interested in my input, but I don't believe I'm the most qualified person on this topic. I did a little digging, and it looks like Pat would have the necessary context. Would you be comfortable inviting Pat rather than me?"

- "Given that this is a decision-making meeting, I think it's more appropriate to have my manager represent our team."

- "Thanks for the invite to this meeting. I don't think I'm required at this point. If it's okay with you, I'd like to send José as my delegate."

Can I contribute in advance?

If the meeting failed your third criteria (you determined that it was an important topic on which you could add unique value, but attending the meeting doesn't fit with your schedule or priorities), consider adding value in advance. Take a few minutes to pull together some notes and to brief the chair or a suitable participant. That will be much more efficient than attending the entire meeting. You can respond to the organizer by saying:

- "This is going to be an important discussion. I'm not able to attend, but I will find some time to share my thoughts so you can include them in the conversation."

- "I'm sorry that I can't attend the meeting. If I prepare you in advance, could I ask that you represent my ideas at the meeting?"

Can I attend only part of the meeting?

If one or more agenda items meets all three of your criteria but others don't, you might have the option of attending only part of the meeting. Respond with one of the following approaches:

- "Thanks for the invite. I think it's really important for me to be part of the discussion on rebranding. Given a few other priorities at the moment, I'm going to excuse myself once that item is complete."

- "Would it be possible to cover the rebranding discussion as the first agenda item? I can't stay for

> the entire meeting but I'd really like to contribute on that one."

Regardless of which option you choose, you're trying to do three things. First, model deliberateness about the use of time. Second, share your rationale so that the meeting organizer has some context for why you're not participating. Third, make an effort to meet the organizer's needs, even if it's not in the way they had originally envisioned.

It might be a bit of a culture shock at first, but all the overwhelmed people with 35 hours a week of meetings will quickly admire your discipline, and you may find folks declining your invites based on similar criteria.

Liane Davey is the cofounder of 3COze Inc. She is the author of *You First: Inspire Your Team to Grow Up, Get Along, and Get Stuff Done* (Wiley, 2013) and a co-author of *Leadership Solutions: The Pathway to Bridge the Leadership Gap* (Jossey-Bass, 2007). Follow her on Twitter @LianeDavey.

CHAPTER 17

How to Interject in a Meeting

by Jodi Glickman

How many times have you sat through a meeting with something brilliant to say but without knowing quite when to say it? Or realized halfway through the meeting that your colleague said something completely erroneous? Or, worse yet, found yourself nodding and smiling in agreement while wondering what in the world the discussion was actually about?

Speaking up in meetings—to interject, correct someone else, or ask for clarification—can be extremely intimidating. Having a few useful phrases at hand can go a

---

Adapted from content posted on hbr.org on November 3, 2010.

long way toward giving you the confidence and tools you need to be able to introduce your thoughts and opinions effectively in meetings.

When You've Got an Idea

Often people don't speak up because they're afraid of going on the record as wrong, uninformed, or the proponent of a dumb idea. A great way to sidestep this inherent fear is to depersonalize your idea, putting a question to the group. When you think you might have a good idea but aren't overly confident about it, go ahead and lob in an offhanded caveat, such as:

- *"Have we thought about* . . . getting Steve involved in the PR campaign directly?"

- *"Did anyone mention* . . . the Brealy report? I seem to recall it covered some of the same topics Andrew has raised here."

- *"Another option we may want to consider* . . . is pushing back the timeline until early October."

- *"Is it worth revisiting* . . . last week's minutes from the meeting to review the agreed-upon product specifications?"

The subtext here is that you're contributing to the discussion and adding value to the group—but not taking ownership of an idea or commandeering the conversation. By using a more informal question or caveat, you'll make your voice and idea heard without overstating your commitment to that idea.

When You Disagree

It's hard to disagree without being disagreeable. When the conversation is heading in a direction that doesn't work for you, it may be difficult to keep your mouth shut. Of course, it's your right (and perhaps even your responsibility) to speak up when you've got something contrarian to say; the key, however, is knowing how to finesse your comments so you don't come off sounding like a jerk. Here are a few strategies and helpful phrases to use in those awkward or tense moments:

- **Be blunt.** "I respectfully disagree with that assessment, Jon." Or "My experience has actually been quite different. I found the team to be highly engaging."

- **Be cagey.** "I just want to play devil's advocate here for a moment. What if we were to go with the opposite approach and use direct-mail marketing instead of relying solely on social media efforts?"

- **Be provocative.** "I want to throw out a curveball here and challenge our assumption that we have to take the deal."

When You're Confused

What's worse than sitting in on a meeting and having no idea what's going on? You may have stumbled in late, tuned out at exactly the wrong moment, or simply never known much about the topic at hand—and found yourself falling further and further in the dark as the meeting progressed. No matter the cause, the longer you wait to ask for clarification, the harder it is to meaningfully reinsert yourself into the conversation.

Here are some good phrases to use the next time you find yourself lost in a meeting:

- *"I'm not entirely sure I'm following you. Could you please recap what you just mentioned regarding* . . . the August delivery?"

- *"I'm sure I'm supposed to know this already, but* . . . how many attendees are we expecting at the conference next week?"

- *"I apologize if this is totally obvious to everyone here, but* . . . what does CAFE stand for?"

- *"This may be a dumb question, but I'm still not up to speed on why* . . . we're not using rail instead of truck."

It's best if you speak up in meetings and make your case—whether to push a new idea, correct a misconception, or simply keep yourself up-to-date on what's really going on. You owe it to yourself and your team to contribute to your fullest potential. It's far less intimidating than you might think.

Jodi Glickman is a speaker, the founder of the communication training firm Great on the Job, and the author of *Great on the Job: What to Say, How to Say It. The Secrets of Getting Ahead* (St. Martin's Griffin, 2011). Follow Jodi on Twitter @greatonthejob.

CHAPTER 18

Stuck in a Meeting from Hell? Here's What to Do

by Melissa Raffoni

We've all been in meetings that seem to go on forever, whether they're being dominated by windbags or bounce aimlessly from one topic to the next. Don't just sit there and roll your eyes. Take control by trying one of the following options.

Be brave. Play dumb.

Even if you think you know what's going on, you may not really get it, or you may sense others don't get it. Consider the power of the statement, "I'm sorry, I'm lost.

Adapted from content posted on hbr.org on January 29, 2010.

Can somebody help me understand what problem we're trying to solve and what needs to happen to resolve it? Joe, can you help me out?" The key to the success of this tactic isn't your question. It's Joe. The person you appeal to should be one of the strongest communicators in the room. It forces the group to stop and hear clarification from the most articulate person. It often helps get a group back on track. Playing dumb is pretty smart.

Be a helper. Create shared visuals. Use some technology.

Another great question to ask: "Would it be helpful if I took some notes?" Flip open your laptop, and take notes on a projected screen or in a shared document (such as a Google Docs). This is much better than using a marker and flip chart, which don't allow for good group editing and require transcription. Taking and projecting notes serves two purposes. First, it refocuses participants on what they can see before them, which could be a list of questions, decisions to be made, individual commentary, or whatever makes sense.

Second, if you can sort it out, you can use the documentation to drive problem solving. Framing the discussion with a simple outline, such as "Problem, Objectives, Facts, Questions, Action Items, Next Steps," will help move the team from A to B. Better yet, it will keep the team from wandering off to Y and Z.

Also, don't neglect to wrap up the meeting without committing summaries and next steps to the document. Now, given your efforts, the group has a working document that serves as a reference for next time. It sounds simple, but it works. What's really happening is you're volunteering to do the facilitating that the facilitator has failed to do.

Find the root cause of the meeting's lack of focus, and suggest a solution.

Politely observe that "we seem to be spinning our wheels here," and ask what's causing the endless cycles. Sometimes identifying the reason for meetings from hell allows you to refocus them or call a new one to sort through the problem more productively.

Identifying root causes of bad meetings is not always easy. Here are some common examples of barriers that may be making that meeting interminable and unproductive:

- **Lack of preparation.** Often, meetings get stuck because not everyone (or no one) has prepared. Whether that meeting-prep document is sent out early or 20 minutes before the meeting starts, people may not stop to read it. Other times, someone conducts the meeting off the cuff or tosses out issues for brainstorming. These approaches waste everybody's time.

- **Who has the D?** Just ask the question, "Who's responsible for this decision?" Ask that person if they're comfortable making a decision, right now.

- **The right people aren't in the room.** Save a meeting from droning on by identifying the people who are needed but absent. "We really can't move

99

forward on this without Jane." Then cancel the meeting, and reschedule it with Jane.

Taking some of these steps and saying some of these things when you're not in charge might seem professionally precocious, but they're good leadership and management skills. And if you think you're in the meeting from hell, it's likely many of your colleagues do, too. They'll appreciate your effort to get the meeting back on track.

———————————

Melissa Raffoni is founder and CEO of The Raffoni Group.

CHAPTER 19

7 Ways to Stop a Meeting from Dragging On

by Joseph Grenny

When I got a speeding ticket a few years ago, I was offered the option of attending traffic school in lieu of a
black mark on my otherwise spotless driving record.
I showed up at city hall promptly at 6 p.m., hoping my
educational experience would end at 8:30 as advertised.
The instructor was 25 minutes late and quite disorga-
nized. By 8:15, he was on slide 18 of 123 and seemed to
be just getting into the groove. My heart sunk and I was
quickly getting resentful. At 8:26 he launched into what

Adapted from content posted on hbr.org on April 25, 2016.

promised to be a lengthy story about a multicar accident. I felt a toxic sense of dread and powerlessness.

In 1964, social psychologists John Darley and Bibb Latané conducted an experiment on group powerlessness. Subjects were led to believe they were part of a group discussion about personal problems, when one participant is struck with an epileptic seizure. Darley and Latané wondered what conditions would predict whether the subject witnessing the seizure would either sit passively or interrupt the gathering and take action to help. It turned out that the larger the group, the less likely the subject was to break ranks from powerless peers and leave the room in search of help. This has become known as bystander apathy.

If human beings can act so passively when health and safety are on the line, it should be no wonder that we turn ourselves into victims when the sole risk is an hour or two of wasted time. Meetings are notoriously ineffective, because most participants act like passive victims rather than responsible actors.

Interestingly, even meeting leaders often view themselves as constrained by unstated and untested group expectations that limit their ability to intervene effectively in the group process. They allow dysfunctional time-wasting behavior to go unchecked because they imagine it is the vox populi.

I've made myself a meeting victim more often than I'd like to admit, but over the years I've discovered that if I'm suffering, others are likely suffering too, and it's in my power to do something. There are tactful things I can do to not only take responsibility for my own investment of time, but also to become a healthy voice for the silent majority. In fact, most people silently cheer when someone takes action to refocus or cut off time-wasting activities.

Here are seven of my favorite interventions for stopping meandering in a meeting:

- **Come prepared.** You can organize a chaotic conversation and gain disproportionate influence by simply arriving with a clearly articulated straw position on the topic to be discussed. Don't push it on people, but do offer to share it if others believe that it will help accelerate discussion. More often than not they will.

- **Set boundaries.** Take responsibility for your time. If a meeting is notorious for starting late and running over, let people know when the meeting begins what your boundaries are. For example, you might say, "I understand we're starting late but I have a commitment to the Murphy team I want to keep, so I have a hard stop at 10:45."

- **Trust your gut. Go public. Check with the group.** Notice, honor, and trust your gut. If you're feeling lost, pay attention. If you're feeling bored, take notice. There's a good chance others are, too. Then, tactfully and tentatively share your concern. Don't express it as truth; instead, own the fact that it is simply your experience. Next, check to see if others are feeling similarly. Here's what that might sound like: "I'm not sure I'm tracking the discussion.

We seem to be moving between three different agenda items. Are others seeing that, too?"

- **Restate the less than obvious.** If the discussion is toggling between two or more problems, summarize the topics on the table, and suggest the group tackle one at a time. For example, "I'm hearing points about both whether this is a good investment and when we should make the purchase. I think we've already made the purchase decision and timing is the only question. Is that right?"

- **Ask the question no one's asking.** If a sacred cow is glaringly obvious, ask for confirmation of its existence. For example, "I'm getting from the comments that some of us question the wisdom of the original decision. Is that right?"

- **Spot the weeds.** Periodically point out digressions into unproductive detail or tangents. Everyone in the group is responsible for the group process, so if you say nothing, you're part of the problem (see chapter 10 for more on silence in meetings). Say something to the effect of, "It sounds like we're in agreement about the policy. Rather than wordsmith it now, it might be better to have someone do a draft."

- **Clarify responsibilities at the end.** It's rare that someone in the meeting takes the time to summarize decisions and clarify commitments at the end. This usually only takes 60 seconds but can save hours in misunderstanding and unnecessary future meetings. Even if you aren't running the meeting, you can speak up and ask, "Can we take a second to summarize what we've agreed to and who will do what by when? Maybe I'm the only one who's fuzzy, but I want to be sure I follow through on my commitments."

As I sat festering in my misery in traffic school, I began to suspect I was not alone. I had 175 other classmates who might be playing victim right alongside me. So I checked my gut, went public, and addressed the person running the meeting.

"Officer, I'm anxious to hear the end of this story, but I'm wondering what time class ends."

He looked a bit uncertain. "I thought it ended at 9:30."

I heard an audible groan from my classmates.

"What time were you told it ended?" he inquired.

"8:30," I said.

He looked at his watch. Then announced, "Class dismissed." The cheers were audible. I felt like the valedictorian of the class.

———

Joseph Grenny is a four-time *New York Times* best-selling author, keynote speaker, and social scientist. His work has been translated into 28 languages, is available in 36 countries, and has generated results for 300 of the *Fortune* 500. He is the cofounder of VitalSmarts, an innovator in corporate training and leadership development.

CHAPTER 20

When Your Boss Is Terrible at Leading Meetings

by Paul Axtell

If you think your boss is ineffective at leading meetings, you're not alone. Few managers have mastered the art of meetings, and even fewer organizations have made it a priority. Add to that the fact that leaders are busy—and often don't have the time to adequately prepare—and you've got a recipe for ineffective meetings. The question is, what can you do about it?

Adapted from content posted on hbr.org on May 16, 2016.

Three broad perspectives are available to you in every meeting:

1. You can offer to do things to support your boss in preparing, leading, and following up after the meeting.

2. You have the right to ask for whatever you need to be effective in the meeting.

3. You can choose to be responsible for the experience of other people in the meeting.

Let's look at each of these options individually.

What might you offer to do?

I love this perspective because it allows you to be supportive without making your boss wrong. A key aspect of influence is the ability to state a problem without blaming anyone. Offering to supply elements that may be missing is a powerful way to do this. Here are some things you might offer to do:

- Collect agenda suggestions from the group, and then prepare an agenda for your boss to review and edit.

- Find team members to lead the different agenda items, or offer to lead the meeting so the boss can more fully focus on the conversation.

- Handle all of the room arrangements—and be there early to make sure it's all set.

- Help bring the conversation back when it wanders away from the intended path.

- Notice who isn't yet involved in the conversation, and invite them to speak.

- Take notes so that a written summary can be prepared quickly after the meeting.

- Chart complex conversations on a whiteboard as they unfold so the group can stay on track and see what has been said.

- Listen for commitments and actions that are voiced, and then review them during the closing for each topic.

- Write and distribute a summary shortly after the meeting ends.

Stepping up and offering to do something will usually be appreciated and respected. However, we all know that our ability to speak frankly with our boss is determined by the level of trust and respect that exists between us. If your boss values what you bring to the group, you can be straightforward: "Sam, I think we can improve the quality of our meetings by doing a couple of things differently. If you agree, I would be willing to do the following."

If your boss takes offense at your offer or says, "No thanks, I've got it under control," then respond with, "OK, and if you change your mind, let me know. I just want to do whatever I can to support you." None of us are as open-minded or coachable in the moment as we think we are. There is a good chance that your boss will continue to think about your suggestion during the next few meetings. Without your offer, nothing will change; with your offer, it just might.

What do you need to be effective?

What are your most common complaints about these meetings? What could you ask for that would resolve each complaint? If you need something in order to be both present and productive in a meeting, find a diplomatic way to ask for it. Other people will probably be having the same experience and will welcome your initiative. Here are some suggestions for asking for what you need.

- **An agenda:** "Most of the time, I think it's fine to find out what's on the agenda when we walk into the meeting. On a few topics, like the budget, however, I would appreciate knowing the agenda ahead of time so I can prepare in a way that lets me add value to the conversation."

- **Proper setup for each topic:** "Before we start this conversation, I'd like to know what input you're looking for from us and where you want to be at the end of this discussion."

- **Broader participation:** "I realize we're a bit pressed for time, but there are a couple of people I'd really like to hear from in this conversation. So I'd appreciate if we could stay with this topic a bit longer so Sarah, Ganesh, and Tori can give us their views."

- **Clarity:** "I might be the only person struggling with this conversation, but I need to get clear on where we are with this and what we've said so far."

- **To stay on track:** "It appears that we're now talking about something different than what's on the agenda. Do we want to stay with this new topic or go back to our intended discussion?"

- **Alignment:** "It seems the group has settled on a direction. I'd like to ensure the decision works for everyone."

- **Next steps:** "This was a great conversation, and I want to be clear about what, if anything, I need to do as a result. Could we nail down what actions will be taken next and when we should have them completed?"

How can you affect the experience of other participants?

Usually we go into a meeting thinking about one person: ourselves. Fair enough, but looking out for others is an easy way to add value and impact in an organization.

Consider these questions:

- Who is not yet participating in the conversation who might have something to say or ask?

- Who is affected by the decision and has not yet voiced their concerns or ideas?

- Who might not be able to attend and would like you to take notes or represent them in the meeting?

- Who would appreciate your collaboration on small-group work that is assigned during the meeting?

OK, now it's up to you. This is wonderful place to trust your instincts. Sincerity trumps all conversational skills. Take your boss to coffee, and offer to help. And, try the ideas that resonate with you in other meetings that you attend. You'll be pleased with the results.

Paul Axtell provides consulting and personal effectiveness training to a wide variety of clients, from *Fortune* 500 companies to universities. His latest book, *Meetings Matter: 8 Powerful Strategies for Remarkable Conversations* (Jackson Creek, 2015), received awards from the Nonfiction Book Awards and the Benjamin Franklin Book Awards, a Silver award in the Nautilus Book Awards, and was first runner-up for the Eric Hoffer Prize.

SECTION FOUR

Close and Follow Up

CHAPTER 21

The Right Way to End a Meeting

by Paul Axtell

A common complaint among managers is that the conversations they have with employees aren't producing results. "We keep talking about the same issue over and over, but nothing seems to ever happen!" they say. That's because most managers are missing a vital skill: the ability to deliberately close a conversation. If you end a conversation well, it will improve each and every interaction you have, ultimately creating impact.

Meetings are a series of conversations—an opportunity to clarify issues, set direction, sharpen focus, and move objectives forward. To maximize their effect, you need to actively design the conversation. While the

---

Adapted from content posted on hbr.org on March 11, 2015.

overall approach is straightforward—and may seem like basic stuff—not enough managers are actually doing this in practice.

- **Set up each conversation** so everyone knows the intended outcomes and how to participate.

- **Manage the conversation rigorously** so the discussion stays on track and everyone is engaged.

- **Close the conversation** to ensure alignment, clarity on next steps, and awareness of the value created.

In my 35 years of experience as a corporate trainer, I've found that closure is more often than not the missing link between meetings and impact. Without it, things can be left unsaid, unchallenged, unclear, and uncommitted. Each agenda item should be considered incomplete unless it is wrapped up in a thoughtful, deliberate way.

To deliberately close a conversation, do these five things:

Check for completion. If you move to the next topic on an agenda too quickly, people will either cycle back to that topic later or they'll leave the meeting with their thoughts unclear or misaligned. Ask, "Is there anything else someone needs to say or ask before we change topics or adjourn the meeting?" Giving people the space to address their lingering concerns and questions allows you to deal with those issues promptly and move forward.

Check for alignment. If someone can't live with the decisions being made in the meeting or the potential outcome of those decisions, ask that person what it would take to get them on board. People prefer to be united with the group, and if they aren't, there's a reason behind it that needs to be surfaced. Asking the question, "Is everyone OK with where we ended up?" will surface questions or concerns so they can be resolved as soon as possible.

Agree on next steps. Getting firm, clear commitments is the primary way to ensure progress between meetings. In order for a conversation to lead to action, you need to clearly state what you will do by when and ask others to do the same. To maintain the momentum of any project, nail down agreed-upon next steps, firm timelines, and individual responsibilities, and then follow up often. The question to ask here is "What, exactly, will we do by our next meeting to ensure progress?"

Reflect on the value of what you accomplished. This is one of the most powerful acknowledgment and appreciation tools. People rarely state the value created by a conversation, and therefore lose a wonderful opportunity to validate both the conversation and the individuals who are a part of it. After a presentation don't just say, "That was good." Instead, say "Let me tell you the five things I'm taking away from your presentation."

Check for acknowledgments. Did anyone contribute to the conversation in a way that needs to be highlighted? While you don't want to use acknowledgment and appreciation so frequently that it becomes a commodity with no value, at times someone's questions or remarks do help provide the tipping point that turns an ordinary conversation into an extraordinary one—and that's worth acknowledging. Doing so reinforces the conversations that occurred, supports the people in the meeting, and encourages everyone's desire to produce the expected results.

Try spending the next three weeks working on closing every conversation in this deliberate, thoughtful way. You'll see an immediate impact on how and when things get done.

———————

Paul Axtell provides consulting and personal effectiveness training to a wide variety of clients, from *Fortune* 500 companies to universities. His latest book, *Meetings Matter: 8 Powerful Strategies for Remarkable Conversations* (Jackson Creek, 2015), received awards from the Nonfiction Book Awards and the Benjamin Franklin Book Awards, a Silver award in the Nautilus Book Awards, and was first runner-up for the Eric Hoffer Prize.

CHAPTER 22

Don't End a Meeting Without Doing These 3 Things

by Bob Frisch and Cary Greene

When a sports team finishes a game, they usually don't gather up their gear and immediately leave the court, rink, field, or locker room. The players and coaches take a few minutes for a post-game meeting—a ritual that's just as important as the pre-game warm-up.

Meeting participants can benefit from the same exercise. A quick wrap-up discussion before attendees leave the room goes a long way toward ensuring the gathering

---

Adapted from content posted on hbr.org on April 26, 2016.

achieved what it set out to do and that future get-togethers will also prove successful. Here are three steps to take at the end of each meeting (though you can, of course, dial up or down each component as the situation warrants). Once you've done this in person, follow up in writing.

Confirm key decisions and next steps.

Recap what was decided in the meeting, who is account-able for following through, when implementation will occur, and how it will be communicated. You want every attendee to leave the meeting with the same understand-ing of what was agreed on so there's little chance of any-one reopening the issues later. One client we've worked with preps for this end-of-meeting review by writing on a flip chart to capture decisions as they're made so nothing is forgotten or overlooked. He also notes action items, including who is responsible, when things should hap-pen, and how status will be reported back to the group.

Develop communication points.

If a colleague who missed the meeting asks an attendee "What happened?" the person who went to the meeting should know what to say. So before you wrap up, put the question to the group. "What are the most impor-tant things we accomplished in our time together here?" As the group responds, capture the key points on a flip chart, whiteboard, or shared document, and briefly sum-marize them. Once you have alignment on what should be communicated to others, ask everyone if there are any parts of the discussion that they wouldn't want to be shared. Some information might be confidential; perhaps some ideas aren't quite ready for dissemination. Be as specific as possible here so everyone clearly understands what is off-limits. Then, as soon as possible after the meeting, send your agreed-upon talking points to everyone in an e-mail. The goal of this exercise is not to give people a script to read from. It's to provide guidance on the key messages they should convey and what they should keep to themselves, if asked, so the rest of the organization gets a consistent picture of what went on. After a recent strategy meeting of the top 30 executives at a major technology company, for example, the group decided on these communication points:

- This was not a one-time event but rather the beginning of this group coming together as a senior leadership team.

- We talked about our strategy, which is to build a collection of great businesses in strong categories.

- We agreed that each business should focus on driving its own growth, but where it makes sense, units and functions should leverage each other's best practices and capabilities. We captured some ideas for how to start doing this and talked about opportunities for leaders to grow and take on new boundary-spanning roles.

Gather session feedback.

Especially if your group will meet regularly, ask attendees for feedback on the session while it's fresh in their minds. This is an often-missed opportunity to learn what people liked and what they would change. Instead of asking a broad question like "What feedback do you have?" which often yields equally vague and unhelpful responses, break the discussion into what we call "roses" (positives) and "thorns" (negatives). Start with the latter. Tell attendees to think about everything they have received or done related to the meeting from the time they were invited right through the review, including any pre-reads or prework and aspects of the meeting itself (such as location and use of time). Then ask, "What could be improved?" Avoid debating the suggestions raised, but do ask questions to clarify what's being said. Finally, turn to roses. Ask the group, "What went well? What should we be sure to do again in the future?" Combined with the recap of decisions, next steps, and talking points, this last discussion helps you end the session on a positive note.

When you embed a regular post-meeting debrief that incorporates these three elements into your meetings, you'll help your team dramatically improve its play.

Bob Frisch is the managing partner of the Strategic Offsites Group, a Boston-based consultancy, and is the author of *Who's In The Room? How Great Leaders Structure and Manage the Teams Around Them* (Jossey-Bass, 2012). He is the author of four *Harvard Business Review* articles, including "Off-Sites That Work" (June 2006).

Cary Greene is a partner of the Strategic Offsites Group. They are coauthors of *Simple Sabotage: A Modern Field Manual for Detecting & Rooting Out Everyday Behaviors That Undermine Your Workplace* (HarperOne, 2015) and are frequent contributors to hbr.org.

Specific Types of Meetings

CHAPTER 23

What Everyone Should Know About Running Virtual Meetings

by Paul Axtell

To make sure that your virtual meetings are adding value and velocity to your projects, do three things:

Focus on relationships.

The quality of people's relationships in a meeting determines the quality of the conversations that will occur during the meeting. That's why it's important to set aside time to build relationships among team members.

Adapted from content posted on hbr.org on April 14, 2016.

Start with casual conversation.

Make it a practice for the conference lines to be open 10 minutes early, and designate that time for catching up. Ask someone to be there to greet and talk with people once the lines are open. If you're leading the meeting, prepare ahead of time so that you can spend time chatting rather than answering e-mails or reviewing your notes. Encourage others to make it a practice to show up early to converse.

Then, at the start of each meeting, ask three people to take a couple of minutes to share what's happening with them. Here are my favorite ways to start this brief conversation:

- Please catch us up on one of your other projects.

- What's happening in your country?

- How's your family?

Use people's names.

During the meeting, credit people when you refer to their earlier comments. Keep a chart next to you to help remember who's out there. People love to be recognized, and in virtual meetings, it builds a sense of community that can otherwise be diminished by not being in the same space. It also pulls meeting participants into a zone of being more attentive and thoughtful.

Meet face-to-face.

When team members visit from out of town or from another country, find time to see them. Schedule a working dinner. Invite them to coffee. If there's driving involved, ride together. Pick them up at the airport. This lays the foundation for authentic conversation—so you'll feel less distant on your next virtual encounter.

Prepare, so you can be present and productive.

Publish an agenda.

A clear agenda helps your participants understand how you'll conduct the virtual meeting and allows them to think about and prepare for each topic in advance. This is particularly important for those who speak English as a second language. When people have time to prepare, they can participate more fully and powerfully. Expecting people to develop their thinking and then express it clearly in the moment during a meeting is asking too much.

The agenda doesn't need to be elaborate. For each topic, answer these questions:

- Why is this topic on our agenda?

- How much time is allocated for this topic?

- Where do we want to be at the end of our discussion?

- What do we need from participants?

Give yourself more time.

Plan on 20% more time than you think you'll need for each topic. The process of getting broad participation and checking to see if everyone has had a chance to express their views and ask their questions takes time— lots of time. You don't want to feel any pressure to get through an agenda. You'll sacrifice clarity and alignment if you or your team members feel rushed. You can always end early if the extra time you've built in isn't needed.

Identify who you want to hear from.

Before the meeting, consider:

- Who would get the conversation off to a great start?

- Who will be most affected by the topic?

- Who is likely to have different views and ideas?

- Whose experience needs to be brought into the conversation?

Part of feeling included and adding value in a group is having the opportunity to share what you're thinking about the topic. This can be difficult when you're in the same room and even harder virtually. Once you've thought about who you want to hear from, tell people which topics you'd like their input on. Letting people know that you want broad participation is the first step; calling on people strategically and gently is the second step. Knowing ahead of time who you want to get into the conversation for each topic will make this easy.

Lead to accomplish the agenda and to get broad participation.

Review how you'll manage the conversation.

Virtual meetings require a stronger leadership approach because you don't have access to the nonverbal cues about whether people have questions or would like to get into the conversation. These meetings also require more empathy and thoughtfulness on your part because people have this sense of being less connected than when they're in the same room.

Ask for the permission you need to be able to relax and enjoy leading the meeting. This is what I usually request:

- Permission to be firm about keeping the conversation on track

- Freedom to call on different people when it seems appropriate

- Agreement from everyone about setting aside their technology, unless they have a good reason for keeping it available

I also let people know that while I have a plan for the meeting, I'm open to their coaching and ideas on making the meeting work for everyone.

Asking for what you want gives you the opportunity to guide the group without making anyone wrong. It also gives people in the group permission to step outside of their normal ways of interacting and participate authentically. It's easy to be ourselves in small groups of four or five people over coffee. In larger groups and virtual groups, the conversation needs to be set up to be safe and effective.

Consider covering these points in your opening:

- "With your permission, I'd like to manage our conversation today in a deliberate fashion so that we all stay on track and to make sure that everyone gets heard. This doesn't mean that I intend to be heavy-handed; I'd just like more freedom to keep the conversation focused and permission to call on people to ensure we have everyone's questions and views expressed before we end a topic."

- "For each item, I'd like to ask certain people to start the topic off. I've made notes on who I think might be affected and will check with each of you. Of course, if I haven't called on you and you want to add something, please do so. You always have permission to get into any conversation if your ideas, questions, and views have not yet been expressed."

Then, manage the conversation thoughtfully.

Go slowly. Without being able to see people as they speak, it's not only harder to hear, it's more difficult to process what's being said. Speaking succinctly will help, and a calmer pace will provide openings for people to ask their questions. Refer to your chart of who's in the meeting to keep track of who's already spoken and to remind you to invite others to add to the conversation.

Consider adding a process step to check for clarity on each topic. Without visual clues, you can't always tell when people aren't understanding or are disagreeing. If you have people with different language or cultural backgrounds, getting to clarity and alignment may require more time going back and forth.

———————

Paul Axtell provides consulting and personal effectiveness training to a wide variety of clients, from *Fortune* 500 companies to universities. His latest book, *Meetings Matter: 8 Powerful Strategies for Remarkable Conversations* (Jackson Creek, 2015), received awards from the Nonfiction Book Awards and the Benjamin Franklin Book Awards, a Silver award in the Nautilus Book Awards, and was first runner-up for the Eric Hoffer Prize.

CHAPTER 24

How to Run a Great Virtual Meeting

by Keith Ferrazzi

Virtual meetings have the potential to be more valuable than traditional face-to-face meetings. Beyond the fact that they're an inexpensive way to get people together— no travel costs and readily available technology—they're also a great opportunity to build engagement, trust, and candor among teams.

Virtual meetings are just as effective as in-person gatherings if key rules and processes are maintained and respected. Here's my comprehensive list of simple steps you can take to get the most out of your next one.

Adapted from content posted on hbr.org on March 27, 2015.

Before the Meeting

Turn the video on.

Since everyone on the call is separated by distance, using video is the best thing you can do to make everyone feel like they're in the same room. Choose from several options, including WebEx and Skype. Video makes people feel more engaged because it lets team members see each other's emotions and reactions, which immediately humanizes things. No longer are they just voices on a phone line; they're the faces of your coworkers responding to what you and others are saying. Without video, you'll never know if the dead silence in a virtual meeting is happening because somebody isn't paying attention, someone's rolling their eyes in exasperation, or an individual is nodding their head in agreement. Facial expressions matter.

Cut out status updates.

Too many meetings, virtual and otherwise, are reminiscent of a bunch of fifth graders reading to each other around the table: a waste of the valuable time and opportunity of having people together. The solution is to send out a simple half-page document in advance of the meeting to report on key agenda items—and then only spend time on it in the meeting if people need to ask questions or want to comment.

This type of prework prepares participants to take full advantage of the meeting by thinking ahead about the content, formulating ideas, or getting to know others in the group. This can help keep team members engaged, says business consultant Nancy M. Settle-Murphy in her book *Leading Effective Virtual Teams*. But one thing is critical: It has to be assumed that everyone has read the pre-reading. Not doing so becomes an ethical violation against the team. I use the word "ethical" because it's stealing time from the team—and that's a disrespectful habit. The leader needs to aggressively set the tone that the pre-reading should be done in advance of the meeting.

Come prepared with the team's opinions.

Not only do you need to do your pre-reading, but after seeing the agenda, you should also discuss what's going to be covered with your team—that is, do your own due diligence. Often people get on a virtual call with a point of view, but because they haven't done any real homework beforehand, they end up reversing their opinions once the call has ended and they've learned new information that they could have easily obtained in advance. If there's a topic that seems to have interdependencies with people who work in another location, get their input ahead of time so you're best representing those constituents in the meeting.

During the Meeting

Encourage collaborative problem solving.

Replace the standard detailed status updates that can weigh meetings down with a group problem-solving session. How do they work? Raise a topic for discussion, and the team works together—viewing their fellow team members as sources of advice—to unearth information and viewpoints and to generate fresh ideas in response to business challenges.

Give each person time on the agenda.

Along with collaborative problem solving, giving each person time on the agenda fosters greater collaboration and helps all team members weigh in. Here's how it works: In advance of the session, have team members write up an issue they've been struggling with and bring it to the group, one at a time. Each team member then gets five minutes on the agenda to discuss their issue. The group then goes around the table so everyone gets a chance to either ask a question about it or pass. After the team member answers everyone's questions, people then get an opportunity to offer advice in the "I might suggest" format, or pass. Then you move on to the next issue until everyone has had the opportunity to present their challenge and receive ideas for addressing it.

Kill mute.

In an in-person meeting, there are social norms: You don't get up and walk around the room, not paying attention. Nor do you make a phone call and "check out" from the meeting. Virtual meetings should be no different. You can't press mute and leave the room to get something or strike up a conversation with your spouse. So establish a standard: Just because you're in a virtual meeting and it's possible to be disrespectful without others knowing, such behavior is unacceptable. If you wouldn't do something in person, don't do it virtually.

Turning the volume on for everyone's phones will keep people in line and raises the potential for lively discussion, shared laughter, and creativity.

Ban multitasking.

Once thought of as a way to get many things done at once, multitasking is now understood to be a way to do many things poorly. Science shows us that despite the brain's remarkable complexity and power, there's a bottleneck in information processing when it tries to perform two distinct tasks at once. Not only is this bad for your brain, it's bad for your team. Set a firm policy that multitasking during your meeting is unacceptable, as it's important for everyone to be mentally present.

Here are three ways to make sure the ban on multitasking is followed:

- **Use video.** It essentially eliminates multitasking, because your colleagues can see you.

- **Call on specific people.** Ask someone, by name, to share their thoughts. Since no one likes to be caught off-guard, they'll be more apt to pay attention.

- **Give people different tasks in the meeting.** To keep people engaged, have a different team member keep the minutes of the meeting each time; track action items, owners and deadlines; and try coming up with a fun question to ask everyone at the conclusion of the meeting. If you meet regularly, rotate assignments to keep things fresh.

Check in.

Nick Morgan, president of consulting company Public Words, recommends having constant touch points. "In a virtual meeting, you need to stop regularly to take everyone's temperature. And I do mean everyone. Go right around the list, asking each locale or person for input."

Assign a Yoda.

Candor is difficult even for co-located teams, but it's the number one gauge of team productivity. To keep people engaged during virtual meetings, appoint a "Yoda." Like the wise Jedi master in *Star Wars*, the Yoda keeps team members in line and makes sure everyone stays active and on topic. By being courageous and calling out any inappropriate behaviors, the Yoda keeps honesty from boiling over into disrespect. At critical points during the meeting, the leader should turn to the Yoda and ask, "So, what's going on here that nobody's talking about?" This allows the Yoda to express what they see happening and encourage risk-taking.

After the Meeting

Formalize the watercooler.

Have you ever been in a meeting, and after it's over everybody walks out and vents their frustrations next to the water cooler? Make the water cooler conversation the formal ending of your next virtual meeting. Roughly 10 minutes before the meeting ends, do what everybody would have done after the physical meeting—but do it *in* the meeting and make sure it's transparent and conscious, reflecting people's real feelings.

How? Have everyone go around and say what they would've done differently in the meeting. This is the final Yoda moment—the chance to "speak now or forever hold your peace." This is the time when you say what you disagreed with, what you're challenged with, what you're concerned about, what you didn't like, and so on. Make it clear that all the watercooler–type conversations need to happen right now or never happen again. And if they do happen later, you're violating the ethics of the team.

Most important, civility and respect must be the norm in virtual meetings. There must be inalienable ethical rules that you follow before, during, and after a virtual meeting if it is to be truly successful. And that means adhering to two fundamental principles: Be respectful of others' time, and be present.

———————

Keith Ferrazzi is the CEO of Ferrazzi Greenlight, a research-based consulting and training company, and the author of *Who's Got Your Back* (Broadway Books, 2009).

CHAPTER 25

Conduct a Meeting of People from Different Cultures

by Rebecca Knight

When you're running a meeting with participants from different cultures, consider your colleagues' various needs and approaches. How do you brainstorm ideas, make decisions, and address conflict in a way that is comfortable for everyone? Which culture's preferences should be the default? And how can you be sure that people who aren't from the dominant culture participate and are heard?

Adapted from content posted on hbr.org on December 4, 2015.

What the Experts Say

Multicultural meetings can be challenging to lead. "People bring their cultural baggage with them wherever they go—and that includes the workplace," says Jeanne M. Brett, professor of dispute resolution and negotiations at Northwestern University's Kellogg School of Management. Communication styles vary from culture to culture, as do notions of authority and hierarchy, which only heightens the potential for misunderstanding and hard feelings. "If you don't prepare for cultural differences and anticipate them at the front end, they're a lot harder to deal with after the fact," she says. It's daunting, but you needn't feel overwhelmed, says Erin Meyer, a professor at INSEAD and the author of the book *The Culture Maps*. Approach your cross-cultural meeting with an open mind. And have faith in your abilities, because "you likely have more experience than you know," adds Andy Molinsky, professor of organizational behavior at Brandeis University International Business School and the author of the book *Global Dexterity*. "You've probably run meetings where there was quite a lot of diversity, be it gender diversity, functional diversity, seniority diversity, or just different personalities. Culture is one more element," he says. Here are some ideas to help your multicultural meetings go smoothly.

Be mindful of differences . . .

The key to showing cultural sensitivity in the workplace is being aware of the variations that exist among cultures and how they play out, says Molinsky. "There are differences in how and where people are supposed to sit in meetings, the extent to which they get down to business at the start of a meeting versus how much time they spend socializing, the extent to which they're willing to provide feedback or argue publicly—there are so many different elements." Meyer recommends "learning as much as you possibly can about the people and the regions of the world you are collaborating with so that you can adjust your management style in small ways." Study up on a country's customs and professional practices, and become an expert observer of others. It's a team effort. Provide your colleagues with reading material on cultural differences, and encourage colleagues to "think about how their behavior is viewed so they can make adjustments too," she adds.

. . . But don't obsess over them

And yet, says Molinsky, "sometimes culture matters, sometimes it doesn't, and you can't always anticipate" how cultural differences will play out. It's important to respect cultural norms, but don't be rigid about them—and especially don't pigeonhole individuals and groups of people. "Culture is only one potential influence on a person's style, his behavior, and how he perceives things," he says. "You should have a working hypothesis but test it against evidence." As the person in charge of the meeting, you'll probably need to make some adjustments and adaptations to your leadership style, but stay true to yourself, too. Don't be boorish or ignorant, but don't pretend to be someone you're not.

Set expectations

It's important to "create protocols and establish norms at the beginning" of your meetings, says Brett. "You want to be clear about what you expect and how meetings will run," she says. "This gives certain people the freedom to move outside their comfort zone, and it also gives you the freedom to rein in others." Say, for instance, some of your colleagues come from a culture where punctuality is not adhered to, but you want meetings to start and end in a timely manner. "You need to demonstrate that you understand different cultural behavior but also explain why you think it's critical for people to show up to meetings on time—and that people [who are late] will suffer the consequences," says Molinsky. "Be explicit. There are deal breakers." Structure and protocol "can override or supersede cultural norms" in other ways, too. If, for instance, you want to hold a group brainstorming session but some of your colleagues are from a culture that's typically reticent, ensure participation by asking "everyone to go around the room and spend two minutes describing their point of view on a particular problem," he says. "Institute rules" that are clear and that everyone follows.

Build relationships

Getting to know the personalities on your team is sound management practice in any culture, but it's especially important when your team is made up of people from different countries. "You need to know the people on your team and figure out the extent to which culture is an issue for each individual," says Molinsky. Say, for instance, one of your team members comes from a hierarchical culture and is loath to provide feedback to a senior colleague. "If you would like him to speak up in a meeting, you need to talk with him beforehand and strategize with him on how he can adapt his behavior," he says. Alternatively, "you need to forgive him for not doing it." Focus, too, on forging bonds and fostering trust among your team members, says Meyer. "Invest time up front on building emotional bonds so that people on your team have opportunities to get to know each other by sharing meals or talking over drinks," she says. "That way a lot of the cultural differences [that appear in the workplace] won't matter as much."

Be creative with conflict

When it comes to professional meetings, one of the biggest cultural differences is the degree to which open debate and disagreement are viewed as a positive, according to Meyer. "In countries like Korea, Indonesia, and Thailand, saying: 'I disagree,' is seen as very aggressive and could lead to a break in the relationship, whereas in France and Russia, it's seen as a great opportunity to build a relationship," she says. While "individual adjustments like softening your language" can be effective, it's also worth trying to make your team more comfortable with conflict. Meyers suggests that before the meeting, you ask your team members to e-mail their ideas and thoughts to a central organizing body that will be grouped by theme and shared when everyone is together. "That way you're disagreeing with an idea, not a colleague," she says. "It's not personal."

Be flexible

Meetings are only one element of the flow of workplace decision making. There are pre-meetings, post-meetings, informal, one-on-one conversations in the corridor, and impromptu group discussions. If cultural differences are making group meetings particularly challenging, try "soliciting coworkers' opinions in other venues and giving people an opportunity to provide feedback in different ways," says Molinsky. "Be flexible about the process," says Brett. "Consider breaking up your group into smaller subgroups." And remember, adds Meyer, "In many countries, the formal meeting is not the place to hash out ideas—it's for putting a stamp on what we've already decided in pre-meetings," she says. In other words, don't put too much stock in what takes place in the conference room. "Recognize that in many cultures the tough stuff is done off-line, one-on-one."

Consider rewards

"It's really hard for people to overcome their cultural behaviors because they're so ingrained," says Brett. But if you're concerned that cultural differences are having a negative impact on your team's capacity for growth and change, think about ways to push your colleagues outside their cultural comfort zones during meetings. "You need to institutionalize rewards around what you're trying to motivate people to do so that it's hardwired in," says Molinsky. Say, for instance, you want to encourage more-open conflict and feedback at meetings, but your workforce is conflict averse. In that case, you could "make providing feedback part of their performance evaluations" and a prerequisite for promotion. They get rewards when they do it well and perhaps even penalties if they fail. It's not easy, but "it's definitely possible to encourage and train people to behave in ways that might not feel natural," says Meyer.

Rebecca Knight is a freelance journalist based in Boston and a lecturer at Wesleyan University. Her work has been published in the *New York Times, USA Today,* and the *Financial Times.*

CHAPTER 26

Making Global Meetings Work

by June Delano

Running a virtual team is an interesting challenge, especially if people are spread across countries and time zones and have different levels of language proficiency. At one time I had a team of about 17 people spread across 10 countries, and we needed to have a meeting weekly or at least every other week. The challenge was that somebody was always in the meeting in the middle of the night, somebody was always the only person in a room while other people were in small groups.

This content originally appeared in the Virtual Teams module of *Harvard ManageMentor* (product #6789AR).

So we experimented and came up with a model we called "inconvenience everybody equally." That meant that we rotated our meeting time so that at some point, everyone—whether they were in London, Berlin, New Delhi, or New York—was up in the middle of the night or in the middle of their normal workday. And it meant that everybody got a chance to be drowsy and falling asleep, as well as wide awake and full of energy at the peak of their day.

We also came up with a rule that, at first, was very hard to enforce: Even if there were several people in one location, each needed to be on the phone separately—not in a room together. It completely changes the dynamic of a meeting if some people are together in one place and can see and talk to one another off-line.

So although several of us were sitting in a row in cubicles in the same office, we made sure that we all got on the phone equally with everybody else. That meant no side conversations and that everybody needed to put their expression into their voice rather than rely on facial expressions.

We also learned that it was really important to have an agenda go out ahead of time, particularly when you have people who are speaking a second or a third language. Seeing the agenda in advance gave them a chance to read and get familiar with the content and what was going to be discussed.

Finally, we made sure that we kept the agenda to those things that really mattered to everyone who was on the phone. If there are 17 people on the line, you don't want to have people getting bored and losing their sense of involvement and engagement in the meeting.

———————

June Delano is a managing partner and cofounder of The ClearLake Group.

CHAPTER 27

Give Your Standing Meetings a Makeover

by Martha Craumer

Regularly scheduled meetings (staff meetings, progress report meetings, and sales meetings) sometimes seem to be called out of habit or a sense of duty rather than need. They're valuable not only for the information they allow people to share but also for the face time they offer. However, their importance doesn't necessarily make them interesting. Meeting with the same people in the same room every week to discuss the same topics can get boring, resulting in many empty chairs—and a lack of enthusiasm among the remaining attendees. Here are

Adapted from the "The Effective Meeting: A Checklist for Success," *Harvard Management Communication Letter* (reprint #C0103A), March 2001.

some ways to keep your regular meetings fresh—and attendance high.

Regularly review the meeting's purpose

From time to time remind participants of the reasons for meeting, and ask if the meeting still serves that purpose. For example, a project team may hold twice-weekly status reports at the beginning of a project, when there are a lot of new developments and many decisions to make. Once the initial frenzy subsides, though, there may only be enough new information to warrant a monthly meeting.

Solicit agenda items from the group in advance

This gives attendees a chance to bring up issues that are of interest to them.

Cancel when there is no reason to meet

Nothing on the agenda? Don't meet. There's no sense in gathering together just because it's what you do on Tuesdays at 11 a.m. People will come to appreciate that your meetings won't be a waste of time.

Rotate leadership of the meeting

Have each attendee take a turn running the meeting—setting the agenda, preparing materials, and introducing topics. It's a great way to inspire ownership of the meeting.

———

Martha Craumer is a senior writer at The Boston Consulting Group.

CHAPTER 28

How to Do Walking Meetings Right

by Russell Clayton, Christopher Thomas, and Jack Smothers

Fran Melmed is the founder of Context, a communication and change management consulting firm. She spends her days performing communication audits for organizations and meeting with clients. Sounds like a recipe for a sedentary workday, right? On the contrary. Fran is part of a growing trend known as walking meetings or "walk and talk."

A walking meeting is simply that: a meeting that takes place during a walk instead of in an office, board-

---

Adapted from content posted on hbr.org on August 5, 2015.

room, or coffee shop. Nilofer Merchant wrote in *Harvard Business Review* about her own transition to walking meetings after realizing that, like many Americans, she was sitting way too much while she worked. Merchant traded her coffee shop meetings for walking meetings and immediately saw the benefits. Likewise, Melmed finds that merely holding some of her meetings while walking has given her the necessary time to "unplug" that she needs in order to be an effective writer.

Recent research finds that the act of walking leads to increases in creative thinking. This certainly supports the idea that walking meetings are useful. Plenty of anecdotal evidence also suggests that walking meetings lead to more honest exchanges with employees and are more productive than traditional sit-down meetings.

Based on this, we undertook an exploratory study of the benefits associated with walking. We surveyed a population of approximately 150 working adults in the United States to gather input about their walking meeting and work habits. In short, we found that those who participate in walking meetings are 5.25% more likely to report being creative at their jobs than those who do not. Additionally, the responses suggest that walking meetings support cognitive engagement—or focus—on the job. Those who participate in walking meetings are 8.5% more likely to report high levels of engagement.

What we found adds support to the notion that walking meetings are beneficial for workers. Is an increase in creativity of 5.25% likely to make or break a business? Probably not. But look at these findings through the lens of a cost-benefit analysis. The costs associated with regularly participating in walking meetings are next to nil. Keep in mind that walking meetings are *not* breaks from work. They are meetings that would have taken place regardless of whether they were held in someone's office or while walking around your building complex. There may be no cheaper way to achieve moderate increases in creativity and engagement.

Just how do walking meetings produce these positive benefits in the workplace? Ted Eytan, a physician and medical director of the Kaiser Permanente Center for Total Health and a vocal advocate of walking meetings, has some ideas. First, from a neurochemical perspective, Eytan emphasizes that our brains are more relaxed during walks due to the release of certain chemicals. This aids executive function, which governs how we focus on tasks and deal with unforeseen events, among other things. Open-ended responses to our survey seemed to back this up in that people said they had moments of creativity sparked by walking meetings.

Furthermore, Eytan believes walking meetings lead to better employee engagement by breaking down barriers between supervisor and subordinate or between coworkers. He sees the bonding achieved through walking meetings as a micro version of the connection often made between coworkers who travel together on business trips. David Haimes, a senior director of product development at Oracle, has experienced this in his meetings with team members: "The fact that we are walking side by side means the conversation is more peer to peer than when I'm in my office and they're across a desk from me, which reinforces the organizational hierarchy."

To be sure, walking meetings aren't always the right choice (and not everyone is physically able to participate in them). Sometimes it is valuable to have materials or a whiteboard close at hand, and sometimes, as in an intense negotiation, it is important to be face-to-face. The best choices for walking meetings are situations in which colleagues are conferring on decisions or exploring possible solutions. Indeed, in our survey, participants who held managerial and professional positions experienced more of a creativity boost from walking meetings than those in technical or administrative jobs (though all categories realized some benefits).

If you are inspired to give walking meetings a try, here are a few tips that can help your walking meeting go well:

Consider including an "extracurricular" destination on your route.

Eytan, whose office is located in Washington, D.C., often mentions the nearby Washington Coliseum as a place to stroll by and notes it's where the Beatles played their first U.S. concert. Naming a point of interest, he says, provides more rationale and incentive for others to go for a walk.

Avoid making the destination a source of unneeded calories.

One of the arguments in favor of walking meetings is the health benefit. However, this is easily negated if the walking meeting leads to a 425-calorie white-chocolate mocha that wouldn't otherwise be consumed.

**Don't surprise colleagues or clients
with walking meetings.**

It's fine to suggest a walk if it seems appropriate in the moment, as long as it's clear that you'll be fine with a "maybe next time." But if you're planning ahead to spend your time with someone in a walking meeting, have the courtesy to notify them in advance. Doing so allows them to arrive dressed for comfort, perhaps having changed shoes. You might also keep water bottles on hand to offer on warm days.

Stick to small groups.

Haimes recommends a maximum of three people for a walking meeting.

Have fun.

Enjoy the experience of combining work with a bit of exercise and fresh air. Our data shows that those who participate in walking meetings are more satisfied in their jobs than their colleagues who don't.

Based on our survey and the clear case to be made for walking in general as a key to good health, it's smart to make walking meetings a habit—or at least to give them a try.

———————

Russell Clayton is an assistant professor of management at Saint Leo University's Donald R. Tapia School of Business. Follow him on Twitter @ProfessorRWC. **Christopher Thomas** is an assistant professor of management at Saint Louis University's John Cook School of Business. **Jack Smothers** is an assistant professor of management at the University of Southern Indiana's Romain College of Business.

CHAPTER 29

Stand-Up Meetings Don't Work for Everybody

by Bob Frisch

Stand-up meetings have become a routine part of the workday in many organizations, mostly due to the adoption of agile and other innovative management methods. These are usually brief daily progress sessions in which an initiative team updates and coordinates efforts. The phrase "stand up" is literal—participants remain standing for the duration of the meeting—and the reason is

---

Adapted from content posted on hbr.org on May 27, 2016.

speed. You want people to rapidly surface issues and solve disagreements. As the Wikipedia entry for stand-up meetings explains, "The discomfort of standing for long periods is intended to keep the meetings short."

While it's hard to argue with the success of agile tactics, it's worth taking a moment to question the wisdom of an organization adopting stand-up meetings on a widespread basis. They don't work for all interactions, and as with anything, treating them as a one-size-fits-all solution can have unintended consequences.

When I was a managing partner at Accenture, our organization and change strategy team helped design a new conference facility for one of our offices. We specifically varied the table shapes and sizes. Some rooms had a large round one in the center, others the classic boat-shaped, boardroom model. We had open-ended rectangles and squares, as well as U-shaped (with the boss typically seated at the center of the bottom of the U) and V-shaped (where the facilitator can move forward to stand in front of the individual participants) options. The reason for such variety is clear: The dynamics of a meeting are directly related to how people are seated relative to the boss, to one another, and to the presenter or facilitator.

Now think about a stand-up meeting, in which there is no rhyme or reason to how people are positioned. And overlay that with physical differences between teammates. Imagine someone who is 5'3" trying to make a point when a 6'4" colleague is standing in front of them, or picture the two debating the pros and cons of a critical problem while standing up. Don't think that's an issue? Then I'd bet you're not 5'3". Remember too that, statistically speaking, the average male is taller than the average female, so height-ism often carries over into sexism.

Consider also a healthy 25-year-old negotiating a difficult compromise with a 63-year-old peer who suffers from a mild heart condition, with the "time clock" for resolution set by the fact that both have to stand for the length of the conversation. The higher stamina of the younger worker could certainly put an unappreciated thumb on the scale in their favor. Attempting to compensate for these differences by, for example, telling the short people to stand in front or offering the older worker a seat while everyone else stands only serves to reinforce these inequalities. Chairs may make meetings longer, but, depending on the layout of the table, they also put everyone on equal footing (so to speak).

I'm not advocating for eliminating stand-up meetings. They can be effective in certain circumstances, and research has shown that they can boost group productivity (see the preface of this book for more on the benefits of stand-up meetings). But any organization that uses them regularly should review how, when, and why they're being held. Is one stand-up per day or week appropriate for your team instead of several? Should stand-up meetings be limited to 5 or 10 minutes or allowed to go longer, occasionally substantially so? Will people really perform better at the desired activity—brainstorming, discussing, decision making, and so on—while on their feet?

Assume you were 5′3″ or in ill health or the most petite female in your organization having a raging disagreement with a tall, young, fit male. Would you want to be standing or seated?

Bob Frisch is the managing partner of the Strategic Offsites Group, a Boston-based consultancy; author of *Who's In The Room? How Great Leaders Structure and Manage the Teams Around Them* (Jossey-Bass, 2012); and coauthor, with Cary Greene, of *Simple Sabotage: A Modern Field Manual for Detecting and Rooting Out Everyday Behaviors That Undermine Your Workplace* (HarperOne, 2015). He is the author of four *Harvard Business Review* articles, including "Off-Sites That Work" (June 2006), and is a frequent contributor to hbr.org.

CHAPTER 30

Leadership Summits That Work

by Bob Frisch and Cary Greene

Every year, in virtually all large and midsize companies, high-level leaders come together for a leadership summit. These events usually last two to four days and can rack up millions of dollars in costs: airfare and accommodations for the 50 to 500 or so attendees, fees for outside speakers, production expenses, the many person days that go into planning, and the enormous opportunity cost incurred by taking so many top managers away from their normal duties for several days.

Reprinted from *Harvard Business Review*, March 2015 (product #R1503F).

When executed well, these meetings are certainly worth the time and expense. They can serve as a powerful catalyst to align leaders, develop solutions to problems, introduce new strategies, and fuel collaboration across the organization. But many companies squander this rare opportunity to harness the collective knowledge of their frontline leaders.

The typical summit begins with a numbing sequence of platform presentations from a parade of C-level executives. Later sessions address topics, such as a new ad campaign or a product rollout schedule, that concern only a portion of the people in the room. A motivational speaker adds a dollop of entertainment. Some breakout sessions and an open mic Q&A with the top team, emceed by the CEO, pass for an exchange of ideas.

Information, proposals, and solutions flow in only one direction—from the top down—and not all that coherently. Attendees leave only slightly better informed and better networked than when they arrived. It's usually not clear whether they've understood the messages they're supposed to take back to their people, much less what anyone would be expected to do as a result. A huge opportunity has been missed. Contrary to what leaders and planners assume, you *can* have genuine and productive conversations with hundreds of people at once. Over the past decade we have designed and conducted leadership summits for thousands of executives in scores of companies, ranging from *Fortune* 500 multinationals to German *Mittelstand* family businesses, and we've seen such conversations take place. Remarkably straightforward strategies and practices can ensure that information flows not only down from the top but also up from the group, and across it, in a way that allows leaders to direct the conversation without inhibiting creative responses. By applying the appropriate techniques before, during, and after the meeting, C-level leaders can get the full value of the knowledge of their frontline executives; see to it that participants leave with unambiguous messages that their employees can turn into action; and transform a meeting that often lulls people to sleep into an event that gets the organization's synapses firing.

Before the Summit

Why do CEOs and their top teams settle for less-than-optimal leadership conferences? A few executives may shy away from a real exchange of ideas for fear of losing control of the meeting. But most leaders and meeting planners simply assume that the events are too unwieldy to allow for much more than an annual update and marching orders from the top.

Here's how the planning process generally unfolds: Some 6 to 12 months in advance, a midlevel executive from HR, finance, strategy, marketing, or corporate communications is charged by the CEO or another top executive with planning the summit. He struggles to get on the executive team's calendar to discuss it. When he does, he uses his allotted 15 minutes to offer up some possible locations, three to five potential guest speakers, and a preliminary agenda seemingly related to a theme. Such themes are often so laughably vacuous—"One company, one vision," "Forward together," "Creating a common future"—that virtually any presentation or activity could be made to fit them. Executive team members spend a few minutes reacting to the locations. They may suggest a few more speakers. And then they promptly forget about the summit until a few weeks before the event, when the planner starts reminding them that they need to pull their presentations together.

That's when people start paying attention. C-level executives, division presidents, and function heads begin lobbying to add speaking slots or favored subjects to the agenda. The planner, lacking any real authority, attempts to allot them all time. Sometimes the CEO suddenly remakes the entire agenda. The result is a highly fragmented or superficial meeting conceived entirely from the perspective of top executives, with hardly a thought given to what the attendees are likely to take away from it, much less what they might contribute.

It doesn't have to be like this. Because these complicated conferences are scheduled so far in advance, there's plenty of time to take the steps needed to create a coherent, focused event. (Table 30-2 at the end of this chapter lays out the timeframe and important milestones for a summit from prep work to post-summit follow-up.)

Assign clear roles that have real authority.

Because the lines between directing, designing, planning, and coordinating a summit can blur, it often turns out that no one is clearly in charge of shaping the event. Roles and responsibilities should be clarified at the outset (see the sidebar "Who Should Do What?"). Rather than viewing meeting planning as a lower-level administrative function, the top executive convening the summit (the "meeting owner") should designate a summit director and grant that person the authority to control the agenda and to say no to people asking to add things that don't fit its focus. Working with a design team, the director should oversee the creation of all pre-meeting, in-meeting, and post-meeting materials and activities. A coordinator, reporting to the director, should be appointed to handle scheduling, travel, production, and logistics with the venue. An emcee should be selected to introduce the sessions and speakers, smooth transitions, clarify questions from the audience to the speakers, and present instant polls and other social media input during the event. Facilitators are also needed to help guide small-group discussions.

WHO SHOULD DO WHAT?

Meeting Owner

- *Who*

  - The CEO or a member of the executive team

- *What*

  - Initiates the meeting and designates a Summit Director

  - Makes final decisions on the meeting's objectives, structure, and design

  - Retains ultimate accountability for achievement of the objectives

(continued)

WHO SHOULD DO WHAT?

Executive Team

- *What*

  - Provides input on the objectives and agenda

  - Develops content with the help of the Content Editor

  - Participates in presentations and panels

  - Tracks progress on commitments made at the summit

Summit Director

- *Who*

  - An internal or external strategy, HR, or marketing executive; reports to the Meeting Owner

- *What*

  - Works with the Meeting Owner and the Executive Team to confirm objectives

  - Owns the agenda

  - Works with the design team to create all meeting materials and activities

  - Manages the planning on a daily basis

Design Team

- *Who*

  - Led by the Summit Director; includes two or three other senior executives

- *What*
  - Creates the detailed agenda
  - Deploys and analyzes all meeting surveys
  - Confirms meeting design

Content Editor

- *Who*
  - A midlevel strategy or communications executive or a third-party speechwriter
- *What*
  - Tasked by the Meeting Owner with overseeing development of content, ensuring that all presentations are aligned with the objectives and coordinated with one another
  - Attends rehearsals and provides feedback to presenters

Coordinator

- *Who*
  - A midlevel event planning or HR executive
- *What*
  - Coordinates scheduling, travel, and lodging
  - Handles venue logistics
  - Coordinates with speakers and other outside vendors

(continued)

WHO SHOULD DO WHAT?

Emcee

- *Who*

  - Could be the Meeting Owner, the Summit Director, or someone outside the company

- *What*

  - Introduces sessions and speakers

  - Creates smooth transitions between sessions

  - Summarizes discussions, clarifies questions from audience members, and presents instant polling and social media input during the event

Facilitators

- *What*

  - Guide small-group discussions in breakout or table sessions

Define a clear set of objectives for the conference by starting with the right questions.

The summit director's first contact with the CEO and the executive team may need to include a discussion of locations—an issue that requires a long lead time. But that's not the most important topic. The director should begin by asking two questions: "What do you want the outcome of the meeting to be from the perspective of the attendees?" and "What do you want them to say when their teams ask, 'What happened at the big meeting?'"

The answers aren't always readily apparent. But after some discussion, most executive teams develop a few concrete objectives. Depending on a company's circumstances, objectives might include aligning everyone around a common set of priorities, solving problems impeding company progress, driving a cultural transformation, or accelerating the integration of a major acquisition. Typically, executives will want to specify several outcomes, but the important point is to formulate them as outcomes, not as a grab bag of agenda items loosely connected by a vague theme.

Take, for example, a consumer products company we'll call Kallos, which has more than 35,000 employees and hundreds of thousands of sales reps. A new leader had succeeded a celebrity CEO, who in his wake left financial problems, low morale, and a culture that tolerated broken promises on the part of managers. The new CEO and his team, wishing to shake things up, developed five objectives for their summit of 200 executives: reach a realistic understanding of the current state of the company, including the need to drive growth; restore employees' faith in the brand; prepare to embark on a cost-reduction program in a way that would not adversely affect consumers; ensure that everyone understood what they needed to do in the near and long term to fulfill those goals; and lay the groundwork to make sure everyone followed through on his or her promises.

Start the conversation before anyone leaves home.

Eight to ten weeks before the meeting, attendees should be surveyed so that the summit director can determine how much time to spend on each objective and identify related issues that should be addressed. To gauge people's current view of the five objectives, Kallos administered an anonymous survey that asked respondents, among other things, how proud they were of the quality and performance of the company's products, how comfortable they would be describing the financial situation of the company to a newly hired employee, and to what extent they believed that managers they dealt with on a day-to-day basis behaved as if they were accountable for their actions. When 90% of the 200 respondents indicated that they were proud of the brand, the focus of the objective "restore faith in the brand" was shifted to "determine how to communicate our pride in the brand to sales reps." Open-ended survey questions included the standard "What's the one question you or your team would like addressed at the upcoming conference?" and "If you were riding in the elevator with the CEO and could tell him the one thing that would most improve the company's prospects, what would it be?"

Design the summit around the objectives and coordinate the content.

Podium presentations, breakouts, and interactive sessions should be not only relevant to the meeting objectives but also coordinated so that together they form a coherent whole. This is commonsensical, but rare. That's because the first time anyone other than a speaker or a few of his reports hears any of the podium presentations is often at the meeting itself.

Focusing C-level and other stage presentations on the objectives and making sure the presentations tie together requires appointing an individual as a single point of editorial contact. This role may be filled by someone from HR or corporate communications, or by a third-party speechwriter, but whoever it is should enjoy the protection of the meeting owner, who must deflect attempts to interfere. Four to six weeks before the meeting, the content editor should begin to assist all presenters, including outside speakers, in using one or more of the meeting's objectives as the starting point and backbone of their presentations and to coordinate the presentations with one another. The editor should attend rehearsals and provide feedback. He must hold the line against presenters who say they have a few extra slides but promise they can get through them in the allotted time and those who try to cram mountains of information onto each slide. With the guidance of a firm editorial hand, hours of formerly "must have" presentations by a succession of C-level executives will be transformed into short, pithy, coordinated talks.

Engage participants in the issues in the days leading up to the summit.

Seven to ten days before the meeting, attendees can be given reading material focused on the objectives. Include only the minimum amount necessary to set up discussions planned for the event. We've found that carefully focused and framed material usually takes no more than 60 minutes to read.

An orientation webcast, similarly lasting no more than an hour, can also prepare participants to make meaningful contributions at the summit. For one luxury goods company, a key objective of an upcoming leadership conference was to prepare the organization for a new global e-commerce division, which would supplant an outmoded regional structure. Before the meeting, participants were required to join in on one of three webcasts conducted by the new division head, who used a few simple diagrams to explain the new operating structure and then answered typed-in questions from participants. Instead of wasting valuable conference time explaining the structure, top leaders were able to have a problem-solving session about its implementation with knowledgeable, well-prepared attendees—the people who would ultimately have to make the new structure work.

During the Summit

Solid pre-meeting work clarifies the objectives, coordinates the content, and initiates engagement with attendees. The design and execution of the meeting itself should make that work come alive in what is in essence a series of structured conversations, carefully orchestrated to generate ideas, alignment, and, often, surprises along the way. Employing some simple principles and tools can make that happen.

Pay attention to the pace and rhythm of the meeting.

Kallos kicked off its conference with a brief (15-minute) keynote in which the CEO introduced the meeting objectives and framed what was going to unfold. Day one was devoted to the first two objectives: understanding the current state of the company and communicating pride in the brand. Two 20-minute podium presentations, each focused on one objective, were broken up by exercises performed by each table and breakout sessions, followed by reports to the entire assembly. During lunch, a guest speaker addressed the drivers of successful direct selling, offered a case study, and took questions from the audience. After lunch, presentations from the product and marketing group, along with several exercises, focused on communicating pride in the brand, particularly to sales reps. Day two—featuring a similar mix of presentations, exercises, and breakouts, and a Q&A with the executive team—was devoted to the remaining objectives: cost reduction, accountability, and commitment. An abbreviated day three included breakouts by region and concluded with a call to action from the CEO and promises from the executive team to track and support the commitments individuals and groups had made during the summit.

IT'S TIME TO BREAK UP WITH BREAKOUT GROUPS

by Andrew McAfee

Does anyone actually enjoy breakout groups? It's a serious question. I participate in more than a few full-day or longer meetings every year—management retreats, training sessions, meetings of centers and professional

(continued)

IT'S TIME TO BREAK UP WITH BREAKOUT GROUPS

societies, and so on—and there's nothing I dread seeing on the agenda more than a time slot devoted to "breakout groups."

This time slot usually follows a presentation on an important topic. The organizers then ask participants to split up into breakout groups for an hour. Groups could be organized in any number of other ways, and participants are typically assigned into these groups randomly. The groups report back for 30 minutes, then everyone goes to lunch.

I find this a complete waste of an hour and a half. For one thing, the random assignments mean that many (most?) people spend the time in a group where they know little about the topic and probably also care little about it. For another, the reporting back is rushed, superficial ("we talked about X, then we talked about Y"), and rarely questioned. And finally, I don't think I've ever seen the results of breakout groups actually used for anything.

I have also noticed that breakout groups are a great way to take energy out of the room. People usually head off to them with an air of resignation and report back from them in monotone.

Breakouts aren't the product of sadistic minds, though. They're put into agendas by well-meaning people who don't want participants to passively sit all day while one person after another drones on at them from onstage. Breakout groups are intended to break up the monotony of a long meeting and get people talking to each other about key topics. These are worthy goals; breakout groups are just lousy at realizing them.

What could work better? I think time slots devoted to mini "unconferences" would. I first came across the concept at FOO ("friends of O'Reilly") events organized by tech guru Tim O'Reilly. At an unconference, time slots and meeting rooms are predetermined, but nothing else is. Using whiteboards or sticky notes, people propose sessions that they want to lead or facilitate and also decide (by looking at the whiteboards or sticky notes) which ones they want to attend. The photo here shows a portion of the agenda for the recently completed FOO Camp.

This agenda was assembled on the fly and reflected the topics participants cared enough about to volunteer their time, energy, and knowledge. Attendance at each session reflected relative interest in the topic among all participants. Attendance varies widely, but

(continued)

IT'S TIME TO BREAK UP WITH BREAKOUT GROUPS

this is not perceived as a problem; some topics are just of narrower interest than others.

I think it would be straightforward to adopt the unconference approach to time slots at corporate meetings. If the organizers had a couple of topics that they wanted to be sure to cover, they could put them on the whiteboard before opening it up to others. And the organizers could wander around the rooms while sessions were taking place to see which ones had the most attendance and energy. Those should be the ones whose leaders report back to the group as a whole.

Andrew McAfee is the codirector of the Initiative on the Digital Economy in the MIT Sloan School of Management. He is the author of *Enterprise 2.0* and the coauthor, with Erik Brynjolfsson, of *The Second Machine Age*.

Adapted from content posted on hbr.org on July 18, 2012.

Allow for flexibility within sessions.

Given the many moving parts of large, multiday meetings—presentations, breaks, meals, breakouts, audiovisual setup, and the like—deviation from the schedule is impossible. Even so, flexibility can be maintained *within* sessions to address issues that arise or to pursue productive lines of discussion. For example, at the luxury goods company's leadership summit, the division president conducted an instant poll asking attendees if they would feel comfortable explaining to others a strategy she'd just outlined. When a large percentage of the 90 people there said no, she asked participants to anonymously submit written questions, which she addressed on the spot. Only after a second instant poll indicated that virtually all attendees were comfortable explaining the strategy to others did the session proceed as planned.

Improve the quality and effectiveness of top-down communication.

During conferences, top-down communication generally takes place in three ways: podium presentations, videos, and Q&As with the executive team. If the editor responsible for coordinating content has done a good job, the podium presentations will be succinct and integrated. We have found that an ideal podium session includes no more than four presenters who speak for 15 to 20 minutes each, using just five to seven slides.

Most leadership summits also include an open mic Q&A session in which attendees ask questions of the CEO or the executive team. The worthy intent is to provide unvarnished answers from the top in response to what's really on people's minds. But what actually happens is wearyingly predictable: impromptu speeches disguised as questions, multipart inquiries requiring time-consuming answers, softball questions intended to curry favor with the leaders, and questions relevant to only a handful of people in the room—to all of which the leaders must extemporize answers. Meanwhile, attendees who are hesitant to raise provocative (or any) issues in front of a large audience remain silent.

There is a better way. If you hold the Q&A on the second day, you can ask people to submit questions at the end of day one. That evening, the summit director, editor, and meeting owner can select the best questions and add ones they feel should have been asked; the executive team can formulate responses to the more provocative ones; and the rest can be parceled out to the appropriate executive team members. Many leaders resist this technique as somehow manipulative or undemocratic, feeling that an open mic is more honest. We argue that, in fact, this approach is ultimately *more* democratic, because it ensures that a cross section of questions are answered in a way that brings substance to what is often an empty exercise.

Use high- and low-tech approaches to capture the thinking of frontline executives and communicate it upward.

Numerous techniques can be employed to harvest the ideas of conference attendees. To determine which tool to use when, the director should ask four closely related questions:

- What kind of input is needed: Opinions? Questions? Brainstorming? Solutions to a specific problem? Complex judgments?

- What characteristics should the communication have: Anonymous or public? Guided or open-ended? In real time or delayed?

- What's the right unit from which to get that kind of input: Individuals? Small tables? Larger break-out groups?

- What are the most effective tools for gathering that kind of input from that unit: Polling? Discussion templates? Worksheets? Complex exercises? (See table 30-1.)

Polling technology as simple as a wireless keypad or an app accessed through a smartphone or web browser allows participants to respond to yes or no questions or to indicate how much they agree with statements such as "I am confident that we will achieve our revenue goals for the next two years." Polling results can be projected at the front of the room in real time for everyone to see (the luxury goods company did this). Text messages work well when more-substantive answers are desired, as when 140 attendees at a leadership conference for an information management company were asked to name the biggest obstacle to the company achieving its growth goals. Among the responses were: "We lack focus," "Too many initiatives distract our attention," "We lack new products," "The plan to grow is not clear," and "Our ability to attract and retain top-notch talent is questionable." The responses were compiled, and a subset was displayed on a screen at the front of the room for discussion.

Such audience response systems can also facilitate highly complex group deliberations during breakout sessions. Take, for example, an exercise we call "the poker chip game," first described in the 2006 *Harvard Business Review* article "Off-Sites That Work," which allows

TABLE 30-1

The right tool to gather input from a crowd

	Response		Participants		Questions	
	Anony-mous	Public	Individual	Group	Open-ended	Pre-defined options
PRE-MEETING						
Survey	●	●	●		●	●
Webcast Q&A		●	●		●	
IN-MEETING						
Question cards	●		●	●	●	
Keypad polling	●		●	●		●
Poker chip game		●	●	●		●
Text-in answers	●		●	●	●	●
Table discussions		●		●	●	
Breakouts		●		●	●	
Pairs		●		●	●	
Com-mitment worksheets		●	●	●	●	
Give and Get		●	●		●	
POST-MEETING						
Survey	●	●	●		●	●
Intracorpo-rate social network	●	●	●		●	

small groups using a game board and some poker chips to determine how a company should allocate its resources. Thanks to technology advances, the results of such exercises can be displayed instantly, providing comprehensive feedback to guide further deliberation.

Kallos conducted this game with its 200 attendees, who were divided among 20 tables. Each table was given 66 poker chips and a game board on which to allocate the discretionary portion of the annual $3.3 billion operating budget. The result was eye-opening for top management. Every table significantly reduced the amount of money budgeted for product development and packaging and increased the allocation for marketing. In the healthy discussion that ensued, a consensus emerged that growth was being constrained by an inability to tell consumers a compelling story.

Many old-school, low-tech tools are still remarkably effective in gathering input, including 3 × 5 cards on which participants write questions; color-coded cards, which participants can hold up in response to questions; templates to guide small-group discussions; and reports from breakout sessions.

Such tools can make brainstorming—often unwieldy and unfocused when conducted with hundreds of people—more productive. Using a technique called "self-facilitated dialogue," Kallos had pairs of participants spend 10 minutes in a conversation, guided by a paper template, about what the company should *start* doing, *stop* doing, and *continue* doing in the next 6 months to implement a strategy for increasing revenue. A member of each pair recorded the results of the conversation on the template. Another template was used to capture the suggestions from all five dialogues around the table and to communicate those results to the entire assembly.

A "round robin" variation of the breakout can be particularly effective in eliciting a full range of reactions to a series of issues. Instead of having 200 people sit through podium presentations on each of the 5 objectives, for instance, Kallos broke attendees into 5 groups of 40. Five executive team members, each responsible for explaining one of the objectives, rotated through the groups. Participants asked questions and provided input on every objective (captured on the lowly flowchart), an opportunity that top-down podium explanations cannot provide.

Make sure ideas flow across the meeting to lay the groundwork for genuine collaboration afterward.

The summit may be the only time in the year when many participants see one another. Yet all too often, connections are left to happen by chance—at meals, in breakout groups, or during coffee breaks and cocktail hours. To connect in a deliberate and more constructive way, we use an exercise we call "Give and Get."

Typically, this exercise is part of a breakout session with anywhere from 30 to 60 people. Two charts, one labeled "Give" and the other marked "Get," hang on opposite walls. On each chart, each participant is assigned a column with his or her photo, name, function, business unit, and location at the top.

In the Get column, each participant posts a card that completes this sentence: "If I could get help in one area that would make me and my team more successful in the coming year, it would be . . ." The card is like a classified ad, asking for a particular type of expertise or assistance. Perhaps someone needs help developing a product feature, reconfiguring a plant layout, or adjusting a customer contract to achieve a certain outcome. In the Give column, the participant posts a card that completes the sentence, "If I could name one area in which my team and I have developed expertise that may be useful to others in the company, it would be . . ."

After all the Give and Get cards have been posted, participants are given Post-it notes and asked to circulate around the room. If a participant sees a Get that she or someone she knows could address, she leaves a Post-it with a message about how she might be able to assist. If she sees a Give that could be helpful to her, she places a Post-it with a message under the card.

Once participants have posted all their offers to assist and requests for help, they switch rooms with another breakout group and survey the Gives and Gets on those walls. If each breakout room holds 50 people, each participant will see 100 requests for help and 100 offers. Those 200 Gives and Gets typically generate hundreds of Post-its, creating a network of connections across locations, functions, and business units. After the meeting, all the Gives and Gets are recorded and distributed to the appropriate individuals for follow-up.

These and other exercises, designed to ripple far beyond the walls of the meeting venue, can be explicitly tied to the objectives of the summit. Kallos, for instance, used a technique called the Wall of Commitments to further its goal of getting participants to follow through on their promises.

Here's how it worked: The packet each participant received on arrival contained worksheets printed on carbonless copy paper. At the end of day one, largely devoted to top-line growth, participants filled out a worksheet that asked them to list specific steps they and their teams would take to increase revenue immediately, in the coming 3 months, and in the coming 12 months. They handed in the original and kept the copy.

During the evening, unbeknownst to the attendees, 200 linear feet of eight-foot foam board walls were constructed in the auditorium. Participants' commitment sheets were posted on the walls under their names, affiliations, and photos. After dinner, the nine members of the executive committee went around the room with a stack of Post-it notes imprinted with their own names and posted comments on the commitment sheets. The comments ranged from "Great idea" and "Let me know if I can help with that" to "This is disappointing" and "I was hoping you were more ambitious than this."

The following morning, when the 200 participants walked into the auditorium, their reaction, as intended, was shock. As they wandered the perimeter of the room reading the comments about their own and their colleagues' commitments, some were visibly embarrassed. During the next two days, the commitment sheets that were generated to address the other objectives—which were added to the walls—became more thoughtful. Not only did the quality of the promised actions greatly improve, but attendees learned what colleagues throughout the organization would be focusing on in the coming months, creating opportunities for collaboration. In several instances, participants formed teams to work on initiatives, coordinate their efforts, or establish discussion groups about commitments that dovetailed.

The element of surprise in this exercise can have a galvanizing effect, and identifying individuals creates opportunities for networking. But both features can be adjusted. For example, to spur ambitious commitments from the outset, participants can be warned that the executive team members will comment on their posts. To avoid embarrassing participants, the comments can be provided to them individually rather than posted publicly. Because Kallos was looking to jump-start a culture change, it dialed up both features.

After the Summit

Because companies generally don't design leadership conferences around concrete objectives, they typically pay little attention to what happens afterward. Morale may have been lifted, but the absence of clear direction usually results in halfhearted follow-up and few tangible outcomes. If, however, you've begun with a purpose in mind, you can do some simple things to make sure it is achieved.

Create succinct materials for
attendees to take home.

The real moment of truth for a summit occurs when leaders return to their divisions, regions, or functions, and people ask, "So, what happened at the meeting?" Those leaders should be able to answer clearly and explain the implications. But that's hard to do if all they've brought back is a notepad full of haphazard observations, doodles, and a few vague slogans, as so often happens. Far better to supply them with communication aids such as talking points, pithy presentations, or video links to drive home the objectives of the meeting and form the basis of discussions with their teams. Meeting participants are encouraged to add their own content to make the messaging relevant. In some cases we have conducted sessions before the close of the meeting in which leaders, working with tablemates, simulate communicating major points to their teams and get feedback on both content and style.

Ensure that all commitments made at the summit—
up, down, and across the organization—are kept.

Answers to all questions that were not addressed at the meeting, whether from executive team leaders or from attendees, should be provided within one to two weeks. What's more, the executive team should track progress on any initiatives or commitments undertaken. Thirty days after the Kallos summit, each participant received an e-mail from an executive committee member listing the actions that person had committed to in the "next

30 days" section of his or her worksheet, followed by a single sentence: "Shoot me a quick e-mail letting me know how these went."

Continue the conversation.

Within 48 hours of the meeting's conclusion, conduct a survey to see if the goals were fulfilled and to ask participants about what worked, what could be improved, and what should be jettisoned for next year's summit. Repeating the pre-meeting survey questions will give you valuable insights into the impact of the event. For example, the percentage of people saying they fully understood the company's growth strategy rose from 37% in Kallos's pre-meeting survey to 82% after the summit, and the percentage describing themselves as "optimistic" or "very optimistic" about the company's prospects rose from 49% to 80%. To encourage collaboration within teams or discussion groups that emerged at the summit, either by design or by happenstance, enable attendees to continue the conversation among themselves through an intracorporate social network.

By adjusting how information flows—more up, more effectively down, and a lot more across—you can turn a leadership summit into a high point of the annual management calendar, one that makes a real difference. Leaders will know in advance that they'll be heard. People across the organization will understand what the results of the meeting mean for them. Executive committee members will know that they're going to get valuable

TABLE 30-2

Countdown to the leadership summit

Objectives	Content	Meeting design and structure	Speakers and presenters	Logistics
4–6 Months				
Begin conversations on desired outcomes.		Appoint Summit Director and assemble design team.	Identify potential outside speakers.	Select venue and finalize dates.
90 Days				
Discuss potential objectives.	Determine required materials for pre-meeting readings and summit presentations.	Determine topics and sequencing.	Secure outside speakers.	Send meeting invites. Finalize travel arrangements.
60 Days				
Solicit input on potential objectives from key stakeholders.	Hold pre-meeting webcast. Deploy pre-meeting survey.	Design high-level agenda.	Determine internal presenters and discuss potential objectives. Select Emcee.	

30 Days				
Establish final set of objectives.	Compile survey results. Draft pre-meeting readings and session material.	Refine structure on the basis of survey results. Draft detailed agenda, including tools to gather input.	Review internal presentations.	Walk through the venue and confirm details, including agenda timing.
1–2 Weeks				
Include objectives in pre-meeting reading material.	Distribute reading material to attendees. Finalize session content.	Conduct final walk-through of detailed agenda.	Conduct rehearsals with presenters and Emcee. Confirm external speakers.	Secure supplies and make table and breakout assignments. Test audiovisual equipment.
During				
Regularly remind attendees of the objectives.	Compile input gathered through breakouts, keypad polls, etc.	Remind attendees of structure and agenda.	Ensure that speakers and presenters understand their roles.	Coordinate ad hoc needs with venue.
After				
	Deploy post-meeting survey. Distribute summit output and other communication aids.	Follow up on commitments. Establish forums for continued collaboration.		

input and that the meeting will be well worth the considerable investment. And enthusiasm will build for each succeeding summit, as people look forward to a memorable event that's strategically significant for everyone.

Bob Frisch is the managing partner of the Strategic Offsites Group, a Boston-based consultancy, and is the author of *Who's In The Room? How Great Leaders Structure and Manage the Teams Around Them* (Jossey-Bass, 2012). He is the author of four *Harvard Business Review* articles, including "Off-Sites That Work" (June 2006). **Cary Greene** is a partner of the Strategic Offsites Group. They are coauthors of *Simple Sabotage: A Modern Field Manual for Detecting & Rooting Out Everyday Behaviors That Undermine Your Workplace* (HarperOne, 2015) and are frequent contributors to hbr.org.

Meeting Preparation Checklist

Use this tool to prepare for your next meeting.

Have you . . .

☐ Identified the specific purpose of the meeting?

☐ Made sure you need a meeting at all?

☐ Developed a preliminary agenda?

☐ Selected the right participants?

☐ Assigned roles to participants?

Adapted from *Running Meetings* (20-Minute Manager series; product #17003), Harvard Business Review Press, 2014.

☐ Decided where and when to hold the meeting and confirmed availability of the space?

☐ Sent the invitation, notifying participants when and where the meeting will be held?

☐ Sent the preliminary agenda to key participants and other stakeholders?

☐ Sent any reports or items needing advance preparation to participants?

☐ Followed up with invitees in person, if appropriate?

☐ Identified, if appropriate, the decision-making process that will be used in the meeting?

☐ Identified, arranged for, and tested any required equipment?

☐ Finalized the agenda and distributed it to all participants?

☐ Verified that all key participants will attend and know their roles?

☐ Prepared yourself?

APPENDIX B

Sample Agendas

A sample meeting agenda

Topic	Preparation	Proposed process
1 **What changes, if any, should we make to the agenda?** TIME: 2 minutes PURPOSE: Decision LEADER: Mike	None	• Mike polls team.
2 **What deltas from the previous meeting will we focus on in this meeting?** TIME: 3 minutes PURPOSE: Decision LEADER: Anne	Review applicable deltas from previous meeting notes.	• Anne reviews areas of improvement that we agreed to focus on during this meeting.

(continued)

Adapted from "How to Design an Agenda for an Effective Meeting," by Roger Schwarz, posted on hbr.org on March 19, 2015.

Topic	Preparation	Proposed process
3 **How do we best manage the fluctuating internal demand for our services?** TIME: 50 minutes PURPOSE: Decision LEADER: Peg	Identify relevant information, criteria, and assumptions that you believe should guide the decision.	• Statement of the problem. TIME: 5 minutes • Team identifies and agrees on relevant information to consider. TIME: 10 minutes • Identify and agree on criteria for acceptable solutions. TIME: 10 minutes • Identify and agree on assumptions. TIME: 10 minutes • Craft solutions that meet the above constraints. TIME: 15 minutes
4 **Which firm should we select for the adjacent markets acquisition study?** TIME: 15 minutes PURPOSE: Decision LEADER: Martin	Read the attached memo recommending three firms. Be prepared to ask questions and share your initial preference and your reasoning.	• Questions and additional information regarding the recommendations of the three firms. • Decision to select one firm.
5 **What developmental assignments are available during the next FY for high-potentials?** TIME: 15 minutes PURPOSE: Decision LEADER: Noah	Review the attached memo identifying the current high-potential managers and the areas in which we are seeking developmental assignments for them. If feasible, be prepared to offer an appropriate developmental assignment.	• Identify the available developmental assignments. • Match the assignments to the pool of high-potential managers. • Agree on next steps for any high-potential managers who have not been given a developmental assignment.
6 PLUS/DELTA: **What did we do well for this meeting? What should we do differently for the next meeting?** TIME: 5 minutes PURPOSE: Decision LEADER: Carrie	None	• Members identify pluses and deltas. • Team agrees on deltas to work on for next meeting.

A blank meeting agenda template

Meeting agenda   MEETING NAME _____

DATE _____

TIME _____

Topic	Preparation	Proposed process
1 TIME ALLOTTED: PURPOSE: LEADER:		
2 TIME ALLOTTED: PURPOSE: LEADER:		
3 TIME ALLOTTED: PURPOSE: LEADER:		
4 TIME ALLOTTED: PURPOSE: LEADER:		
5 TIME ALLOTTED: PURPOSE: LEADER:		

Branded Books Meeting: sales, marketing, production, editorial team

9/17/16; 10:00–11:00; 307W

Jessica, Erin, Lisa, Mary, Jane, Audra, Sarah, Alex, Jen, Kate

Meeting objective:

To coordinate our marketing, sales, production, and editorial activities in order to execute our plan to generate $750,000 in sales of branded e-books across all channels: retail, e-tail, and our own website this fiscal year.

What	How	Who	Time
Introduction	• How did it go? What's the word on the new lines of books?	Mary	5 min
Book revision planning	• Overarching strategy: Need to revise/refresh before a potential customer picks up the book and says, "Outdated!" • Options: ○ Since book display plans are done 4 months in advance, should the reprint schedule be on an 18–24 month cycle? ○ Should we coordinate the revision schedule with the reprint schedule? Do we know the reprint schedule far enough in advance—or is that driven by sales? • Next steps	Jane	15 min

(continued)

What	How	Who	Time
Paperback & e-book publication schedule	• We agreed that we'd offer the e-book and PDF versions of the paperbacks one month pre–bound book date, so the first group of five will be live and promoted on 2/14/17. • How do we develop an informed point of view about e-book/print book publication schedules? How do we gather best practices? • Next steps	Mary	15 min
Pre-sales meeting	• Scheduled for mid-October. • How can the team help prepare? • Should we pursue the possibility of pre-loading the first 10 Must Reads book on an e-reader? • Next steps	Mary	10 min

Merchan-dising idea	• How about grouping our books by topic rather than by series? For example, what if we grouped all of our Managing People books together?
	  ○ *10 Must Reads on Managing People*
	  ○ *HBR on Finding and Keeping the Best People*
	  ○ *HBR Guide to Delivering Effective Feedback*
	• Next steps
		Jane	10 min

Recap	• What we decided • Next steps—who's doing what	Jane	5 min

Meeting Follow-Up Checklist

Have you . . .

- ☐ Written a succinct follow-up note, including what, who, and when?

- ☐ Distributed the note to all participants?

- ☐ Recorded any task due dates in your calendar so you can follow up to make sure they're completed?

- ☐ Distributed the note to all other relevant stakeholders?

Adapted from *Running Meetings* (20-Minute Manager series; product #17003), Harvard Business Review Press, 2014.

- ☐ Followed up with key stakeholders in person to make sure they're aware of meeting highlights?

- ☐ Assessed yourself as leader?

- ☐ Assessed the outcome of the meeting?

- ☐ Met with critics?

- ☐ Thought through what you could do better next time?

Sample Follow-Up Memo

Branded Books Meeting: sales, marketing, production, editorial team

9/17/16 Follow-Up Notes

Attendees: Jessica, Erin, Lisa, Mary, Jane, Audra, Sarah, Alex, Jen, Kate

Meeting objective:

To coordinate our marketing, sales, production, and editorial activities in order to execute our plan to generate $750,000 in sales of branded e-books across all channels—retail, e-tail, and our own website this fiscal year.

What	How	Who	When
Pre-sales meeting	• Most important meeting in the buying cycle • 25 national account reps • Loved the jackets! • Sell sheets very helpful ○ Thanks to Sarah, Mary, and Alex for creating them!	Team	Done
Book revision planning	• Overarching principles ○ When a content area (managing supply chains, doing business in China, marketing) undergoes a sea change, we should be ready to update ASAP. ○ The new content in a refreshed book needs to be game changing. ○ And we must be sure we're going to sell a lot more of the refreshed book; otherwise, we'll lose money on returns. ○ Need to revise/refresh before a potential customer picks up the book and says, "Outdated!"	Jane Jane w/ Mary and Jess	Ongoing Ongoing
Paperback & e-book publication schedule	• We agreed that we'd offer the e-book and PDF versions of the paperbacks one month pre–bound book date, so the first group of five will be live and promoted on **2/14/17**. ○ We agreed that we'd use the branded lines as an experiment for figuring out nontraditional digital/print book release, marketing, and merchandising.	Jane Team	2/14/17

(continued)

What	How	Who	When
Merchandising idea	• What if we suggested grouping our books—all of our books, not just the branded lines—by topic rather than by series (for example, when all six 10 Must Reads are out, as well as the new paperbacks and authored books [such as Grote on performance appraisal]): ○ What if we grouped all the Managing People books together: ■ *10 Must Reads on Managing People* ■ *HBR on Finding and Keeping the Best People* ■ Grote's new book on performance appraisal • In e-tail, we already do this type of grouping (Sarah and Alex); that is, thematic book lists with focus on core topics.		
	○ Need to look at Alex and Sarah's e-tail promotion of *10 Must Reads: The Essentials* with each author's related books.	Sarah	9/18/17
	○ Also need to take a field trip to some physical bookstores—before the winter weather!	Mary	10/18/17

Digital Tools to Make Your Next Meeting More Productive

by Alexandra Samuel

Meetings may seem like the ultimate holdout against the digitization of working life: After all, what's more analog than talking directly with another person? Even though the core work of a meeting—listening to and connecting with other people—hasn't changed, there are lots of ways technology can make that work easier and more effec-

Adapted from content posted on hbr.org on March 12, 2015 and July 3, 2015

tive. Given how much of our working lives we spend in meetings, building a digital meeting toolkit is one of the smartest investments you can make in tech-savvy productivity. Here are the tools you need.

Before Your Meeting

Find a group meeting time with Doodle, which lets you poll the various people who are part of your meeting and find a time that works for everyone. You'll get the best results if you hook it up to your own calendar (so you only offer people options that actually work for you) and if you set expectations by explaining you're using Doodle to find the time that works for as many people as possible—even if you can't find one that works for everyone.

Quickly schedule one-on-one meetings so the process of finding a time doesn't consume more time than the meeting itself. Use Google appointment slots or Calendly to set up times when you're available for calls or meetings, and when you want to take a meeting, share the link to your open slots.

If you're booking a call with someone in another time zone, make sure you're actually booking the same time into your calendars. Send an actual calendar invitation, rather than just agreeing on a time via e-mail, and as long as your calendaring app has built-in time zone support (nearly all of them do), you can avoid making a mistake. And use Every Time Zone to figure out what the time zone difference actually is, so you don't invite someone to a 4 a.m. meeting.

Find a place to meet. On-demand services like Liquid-space or Desks Near Me give you lots of options for identifying a meeting space, even when you're on the road. You can book weekly, daily, or even by the hour.

During Your Meeting

Take notes in Evernote or another dedicated digital notebook application. Capturing good, searchable notes makes meetings much more valuable, and the right note-taking tool will make it easy for you to file your meeting notes with the project or topics they relate to. Best of all, if you use the Evernote mobile app to snap pictures of your meeting whiteboard or flip charts, optical character recognition makes those handwritten notes searchable, too.

Share note taking with Google Docs. When you use a Google Docs document to capture meeting updates in more-or-less real time, you'll be able to see and contribute to each other's notes as long as you have an internet connection. (Be sure to copy the meeting notes in Evernote afterward, if that's where you like to keep all your project notes.) That means you and your team can take notes collaboratively, so that if one person's talking, another person records what's being said. This is a particularly nifty trick if you're working with one or more colleagues on a meeting with a client or another team, because you have a kind of psychic link—you can suggest ideas to one another alongside the notes you're taking. And if you don't have an internet connection but you and your colleagues all work on Macs, you can use the fab SubEthaEdit to collaborate with even less lag than you get on Google Docs, simply by creating a computer-to-computer network.

Bring an extra screen to view reference materials. The one downside of digital note taking is that if you need to refer to a document during your meeting, you have to flip back and forth between your note-taking application and your reference document. That's why I always carry my iPad. I use the application GoodReader to store any PDFs or documents I might need to look at during a meeting. And because GoodReader is hooked up to my DropBox account, I can always access a document I need to have open, even if I didn't think to preload it in GoodReader.

Collaborate with mind mapping. I'm a huge fan of mind mapping: diagramming ideas and information visually, using something that looks like a tree or flow-chart. While some people actually take their meeting notes in mind map form (been there, done that, reverted to text), I find mind maps most useful when I'm part of a group discussion where we need to capture and organize ideas together. My two favorite mind-mapping apps for meetings are MindMeister (very flexible and powerful) and Popplet (less expensive, a little easier to use, less flexible). If you're using mind mapping in a face-to-face meeting, you can simply hook a projector up to one computer, but the real-time collaboration support in these apps mean they're great for using during virtual meetings, too.

Inspire new thinking. Your meeting outcomes will only be as good as the thinking that goes into them. But huddling around a PowerPoint presentation is hardly a recipe for inspiring bold new ideas. Instead, think about using a collaborative visual tool like Popplet to share ideas, so that you can reorganize them on the fly.

Convert action items to tasks. Once you leave a meeting, it's easy for follow-up steps to fall by the wayside. It really helps if everyone in a meeting actually puts their action items into their task manager—something that's a lot easier with TaskClone. A reader put me onto this service, which can scan Evernote to find any action items and then import them into your favorite task management tool.

Access your outcomes. Too often, we leave meetings with a tangible outcome, only to lose it in the digital morass. Even if you generally take your meeting notes in Evernote or another digital note-taking program, you may still have trouble tracking down that brilliant brainstorm that occurred on a pile of Post-its, the inspired idea you wrote in your paper notebook, or the meeting notes written on a flipchart. That's why it's handy to snap a photo of any written output and add it to Evernote, so that it becomes searchable.

For Virtual or Phone Meetings

While all the tools I've mentioned here are useful in both face-to-face and virtual meetings, there are a few extra tools I'd recommend for people conducting virtual or phone meetings.

Share screens faster with Join.me. I've tried GoTo-Meeting, WebEx, Google Hangouts, and Skype. They all work some (or even most) of the time. But the only bullet-proof screen-sharing tool I've used is Join.me. It works for me every time, and because it's so fast to set up a meeting and share a link, it works even if I'm already midcall when I realize I need to share my screen.

Choose a back channel. If you're doing a client or prospect call with colleagues who are in another office or location, keep yourselves in sync by choosing an instant messaging back channel before your meeting begins. There's nothing worse than needing to send your copresenter an urgent note but discovering you have to wait for him to read his e-mail so he can see it. A back channel chat provides a way of discreetly asking someone to let the conversation move forward or of checking in with other meeting attendees to see if they feel like your meeting has lost focus. Your back channel can be Skype, Lync, MSN, Apple Messages, or Gmail Chat—any messaging application works, as long as it has desktop support (so you're not trying to type urgent messages into your phone) and you have connected to your colleague before the meeting begins. (Send a test message just to be sure.) Even if you're using a virtual meeting application that supports private messaging, I recommend using a separate app as your back channel so you don't accidentally share your message with the client.

Record crucial phone meetings. If you're participating in a phone meeting and aren't in a position to take notes (or can't type fast enough), consider recording your call for future reference. TapeACall, which is available for both iPhone and Android, makes it really easy: Just install the app, and then conference the TapeACall number into your call. (Note that in many jurisdictions it's illegal to tape a call unless everyone consents.)

Set up these tools on your computer and mobile devices, and you'll be better equipped to make the most of your meetings. Far from distracting you from your work and colleagues, this is one place technology can help you reconnect with them—by making the time you spend together as valuable as possible.

Alexandra Samuel is a speaker, researcher, and writer who works with the world's leading companies to understand their online customers and craft data-driven reports such as "Sharing Is the New Buying." The author of *Work Smarter with Social Media* (Harvard Business Review Press, 2015), Alex holds a PhD in political science from Harvard University. Follow Alex on Twitter @awsamuel.

Index

Index

Index

Smart advice and inspiration from a source you trust.

If you enjoyed this book and want more comprehensive guidance on essential professional skills, turn to the HBR Guides Boxed Set. Packed with the practical advice you need to succeed, this seven-volume collection provides smart answers to your most pressing work challenges, from writing more effective emails and delivering persuasive presentations to setting priorities and managing up and across.

Harvard Business Review Guides

Available in paperback or ebook format. Plus, find downloadable tools and templates to help you get started.

- Better Business Writing
- Building Your Business Case
- Buying a Small Business
- Coaching Employees
- Delivering Effective Feedback
- Finance Basics for Managers
- Getting the Mentoring You Need
- Getting the Right Work Done

- Leading Teams
- Making Every Meeting Matter
- Managing Stress at Work
- Managing Up and Across
- Negotiating
- Office Politics
- Persuasive Presentations
- Project Management

HBR.ORG/GUIDES

Buy for your team, clients, or event.
Visit hbr.org/bulksales for quantity discount rates.

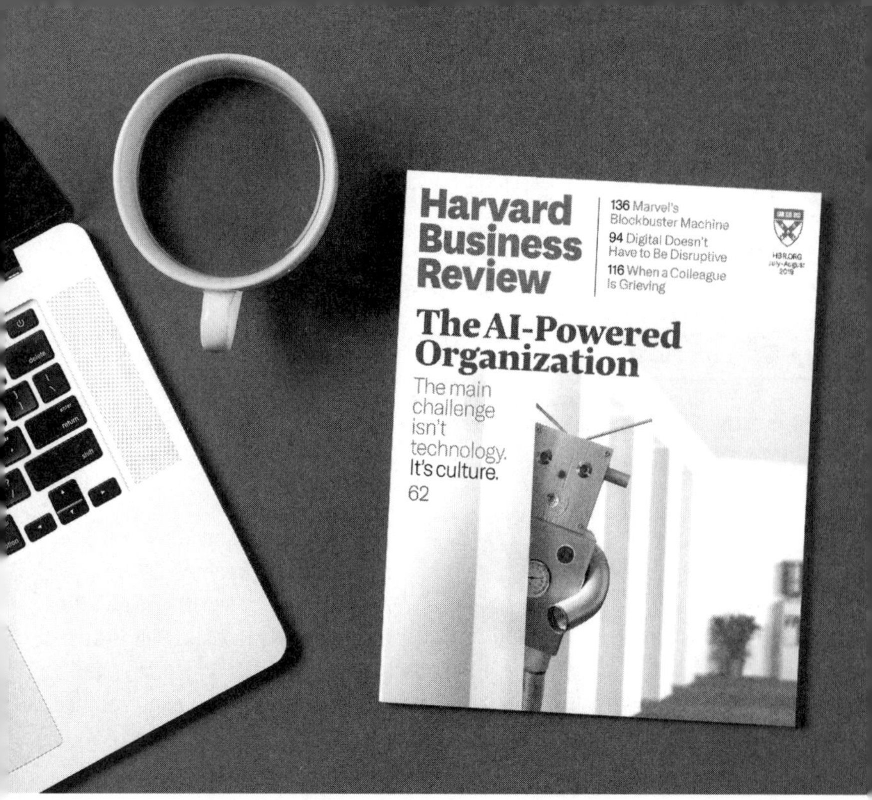

Engage with HBR content the way you want, on any device.

With HBR's new subscription plans, you can access world-renowned **case studies** from Harvard Business School and receive **four free eBooks**. Download and customize prebuilt **slide decks and graphics** from our **Visual Library**. With HBR's archive, top 50 best-selling articles, and five new articles every day, HBR is more than just a magazine.

Subscribe Today
hbr.org/success

The most important management ideas all in one place.

We hope you enjoyed this book from *Harvard Business Review*. For the best ideas HBR has to offer turn to HBR's 10 Must Reads Boxed Set. From books on leadership and strategy to managing yourself and others, this 6-book collection delivers articles on the most essential business topics to help you succeed.

HBR's 10 Must Reads Series

The definitive collection of ideas and best practices on our most sought-after topics from the best minds in business.

- Change Management
- Collaboration
- Communication
- Emotional Intelligence
- Innovation
- Leadership
- Making Smart Decisions

- Managing Across Cultures
- Managing People
- Managing Yourself
- Strategic Marketing
- Strategy
- Teams
- The Essentials

hbr.org/mustreads

Buy for your team, clients, or event.
Visit hbr.org/bulksales for quantity discount rates.